serving and accrediting
INDEPENDENT SCHOOLS

2018 Leadership Retreat

Moving the Rock

Moving the Rock

Seven Levers WE Can Press to Transform Education

Grant Lichtman

JB JOSSEY-BASS™

A Wiley Brand

Published by Jossey-Bass
A Wiley Brand
One Montgomery Street, Suite 1000, San Francisco, CA 94104-4594—www.josseybass.com

Jossey-Bass books and products are available through most bookstores. To contact Jossey-Bass directly call our Customer Care Department within the U.S. at 800-956-7739, outside the U.S. at 317-572-3986, or fax 317-572-4002.

Wiley publishes in a variety of print and electronic formats and by print-on-demand. Some material included with standard print versions of this book may not be included in e-books or in print-on-demand. If this book refers to media such as a CD or DVD that is not included in the version you purchased, you may download this material at http://booksupport.wiley.com. For more information about Wiley products, visit www.wiley.com.

Library of Congress Cataloging-in-Publication Data

Names: Lichtman, Grant, 1956– author.
Title: Moving the rock : seven levers WE can press to transform education / Grant Lichtman.
Description: San Francisco, CA : Jossey-Bass ; Hoboken, NJ : John Wiley & Sons, 2017. | Includes bibliographical references and index.
Identifiers: LCCN 2017026112 (print) | LCCN 2017010696 (ebook) | ISBN 9781119404460 (pdf) | ISBN 9781119404422 (epub) | ISBN 9781119404415 (cloth)
Subjects: LCSH: Educational change. | Educational leadership.
Classification: LCC LB2806 (print) | LCC LB2806 .L46 2017 (ebook) | DDC 370—dc23
LC record available at https://lccn.loc.gov/2017026112

Cover design: Wiley

Cover image: © Martin Barraud/Getty Images-Seesaw, © Jupiterimages/Getty Images-Schoolhouse

Printed in the United States of America

FIRST EDITION

HB Printing   10 9 8 7 6 5 4 3 2 1

CONTENTS

■ ■ ■

ABOUT THE AUTHOR

Grant Lichtman is a globally recognized thought leader in the drive to transform K–12 education. He keynotes conferences and works with school and community teams, helping them to develop their imagination of schools of the future and a comfort and capacity for change. He is the author of two previous books: *#EdJourney: A Roadmap to the Future of Education* and *The Falconer: What We Wish We Had Learned in School*. Grant shares resources, articles, connections with other schools and innovative programs, and his blog at www.grantlichtman.com.

For 15 years Grant was a senior administrator at one of the largest and oldest K–12 independent schools in California with responsibilities that included business, finance, operations, technology, development, campus construction, and global studies. Before working in education, he directed business ventures in the oil and gas industry in the former Soviet Union, South America, and the US Gulf Coast.

Grant graduated from Stanford University with a BS and MS in geology in 1980 and studied the deep ocean basins of the Atlantic and Pacific oceans and the Bering Sea. Grant and his wife, Julie, live in Poway, about 20 miles north of San Diego.

ACKNOWLEDGMENTS

I AM SINCERELY INDEBTED TO THE MANY PEOPLE WHOSE STORIES, VOICES, IDEAS, AND passions formed the basis of this book. I have met, worked with, and gathered knowledge from well over 10,000 educators, students, and community stakeholders in the last four years, and each bit of that work is a small piece of the puzzle I have tried to form. This is their story and vision, not mine.

Having said that, there are smaller groups of people who have given much more deeply of their time and ideas, for which I am truly grateful. Many of them you will meet in the book, so I won't rename them here. I interviewed more than 80 educators and education thought leaders for this book, and most of them are quoted in their own words.

Neil Hokanson, Brad Lichtman, Kami Thordarson, Julie Wilson, and Kelly Young were kind enough to read the manuscript and provide extremely insightful input and advice. And of course, my wonderful editor, Kate Bradford, at Jossey-Bass provided invaluable guidance throughout the process.

There is a group of remarkable, courageous, leading educators in New Zealand with whom I have had the privilege to interact with virtually and in person. There are way too many to name, and I know I will slight some, but Kiwis are so warm and wonderful, they will all forgive me. Among those with whom I have most frequently collaborated are Maurie Abraham, Claire Amos, Becky Hare, Steve Mouldey, and Danielle Myburgh.

A small group of educators and non-educators contributed to the development of my ideas on how virtual reality–based collaborative learning can become radically more accessible to teachers and students right now, not 5 or 10 years down the road. For that work I want to sincerely thank Natalie Bell, Dee Colcord, Kevin Colcord, Andrew Ezokoye, Jill Gough, Maria Guidice, Laura Hazlett, Ann Koufman Frederick, Walter Krumshyn, Michelle Magallenez, Deena Minwalla, David Monaco, Michelle Mullen, Nuket Nolan, Julie Wilson, and Meg Wittman.

Others who are not mentioned in the book with whom I have shared ideas, who helped form the synthesis of the inevitable future of education and the levers that will help make that future a reality include Sara Allan, Pat Bassett, Sara Bird, Kevin Costa, Mark Crotty, Mark Desjardins, Joe Erpelding, Kelly Eveleth, David Farace, Tim Fish, Jordan Greenhall, Megan Henry, Tyler Hodges, Doris Korda, Kawai Lai, Bryan Lakatos, David Leach, Lewis Leiboh, Caryn Lewis, Cassidy Lichtman, Lynn Lillian, Jason Palmer, Stephen Piltch, Megan Powers, Peter Saliba and the entire Tilton School team, Kate Saunders, Jay Scheurle, Kami Thordarson, John Warren, Elliot Washor, Glenn Whitman, and Michael Wirtz.

INTRODUCTION

Impossible is not a fact. It's an opinion. Impossible is not a declaration. It's a dare. Impossible is potential. Impossible is temporary. Impossible is nothing.

Muhammad Ali

The future is here   it's just not evenly distributed.

William Gibson

For four decades I have crisscrossed my own country and visited nearly 50 more. I have shared bottles of bad whiskey with cowboys in smoky Wyoming bars, fine wines with Silicon Valley entrepreneurs, and dirty glasses of bathtub vodka with Siberian oilmen in freezing Gulag-era shacks. I have cast for marlin on a millionaire's yacht and pulled in fishing nets with Filipino fisher folk who just hope for dinner when those nets are set each day. I have broken bread with Hindus in ornate Indian temples, shared seared lamb with Uzbek Muslims, sung hymns in towering Gothic Catholic cathedrals, and held hands in New Age prayer circles. I have friends and colleagues who are rock-ribbed conservatives, wild-eyed liberals, and card-carrying Communists. I have researched alongside leading scientists and parsed biblical cannon with creationist fundamentalists.

There is only one *shared* dream that I have heard from *all* of these people across *all* of these seeming divides: *that our children be happy, successful, and lead lives better than those of our own.* And nearly everyone in every country and every station in life agrees that education is key to the fulfillment of that dream. The value of education is where, despite all that divides us, we mostly come together.

The problem is that education is stuck in a past that no longer exists for our children. This book is about how we unstick it, and the roles each of us—teacher, parent, student, administrator, business leader, foundation director, college professor, president and admissions officer, every member of the community who knows how critical education is to our collective future—can play. Some professional educators, and many others who have grown weary, perhaps even callous, to the seemingly unmovable rock of education, will think the future I describe is wildly improbable, that the calls to action I suggest are scary, unlikely, or a bit crazy. Fortunately, there is a rapidly rising tide of others who know that this future is inevitable and that all we have to do is climb over our fears, find the big points of leverage that are already working in schools and communities around the country and around the world, and *just do it*. We need to stop arguing about the nature of the problem and start building a tsunami of momentum around big, audacious solutions.

Unlike others who have tackled the problems, inequities, and inadequacies of traditional K–12 education, in this book I propose that we *stop fighting the forces that have kept education stuck*. There is another way. I propose we use leverage where we—the large and growing minority of educators, students, parents, community business groups, researchers, philanthropists, journalists, and social media actors—have nearly total control. I hope the levers I propose *are* a bit crazy, because, friends, coloring inside the lines is not working and our kids are the ones suffering for it. We live in a time when we have proven that disruptive innovations can lead to dramatic, positive change; it is time we stop tweaking at the margins of K–12 education because we know audacity works. It is up to us. It is up to you.

> *We need to stop arguing about the nature of the problem and start building a tsunami of momentum around big, audacious solutions.*

Virtually every human institution—economic, social, political, religious—is in a state of fundamental reconfiguration, except education, which structurally is largely unchanged from the highly successful system that evolved during the mid-19th century demand for a population literate enough to fuel the rise of industry, democracy, and imperialism. The current system of education was never designed to deliver equitable outcomes to all learners, nor was it designed to meet the challenges our students will face in a world that is very different from that of the 19th and 20th centuries. Radical change to this outdated system of education over the next generation is inevitable because the needs of our students have changed. Our current model of "school"—students constrained by the industrial model of time in a classroom, knowledge bound up in textbooks, teachers shoveling lessons at students like coal into a furnace, learning parsed into seven prepackaged subjects, students graded and advanced according to meaningless averages—cannot possibly withstand the dissonance between what we *have* today and what our students and our society *need* to embrace the future.

The march of human history has *never* withstood such dissonance over time. The transformation of education will not be even, smooth, or equal. But it is inevitable, it is already happening, and 20 or 30 years is just not a lot of time relative to the increased pace at which human systems have changed in the past. The agrarian revolution took 10,000 years to fully change the path of human history; the industrial revolution 200 years; the information revolution less than two generations. Many thoughtful scientists and behaviorists predict that the "singularity," the point at which powerful artificial intelligence is capable of self-evolution, is less than a generation away. The gap between where education is and where it needs to be to fulfill the basic mission of preparing young people to meet the challenge of *their* future is on us today, and we have a very short period of time to either meet that challenge or watch as our education system, in which we all have so much invested, is pitched into irrelevance.

The Why, What, and How of Educational Change

My head hurts every time I see another article, vodcast, or TED Talk preaching that education must change. That train has already left the station! All of the arguments about *why* education must change can be summarized in less than a sentence, a simple paraphrase of the godfather of modern education, John Dewey, more than a century ago: *The world is changing at an ever-increasing rate and we have to prepare our students for that future, not for the past.* We desperately need to move beyond the discussion of *why* education must change.

Similarly, the question of *what* education must look like in the future, although not wholly formed, is increasingly coming into focus. In this book we will touch briefly on *what* great education looks like now and in the future, but many others have covered those topics with insight, examples, depth, and clarity. I have asked thousands of Americans—parents, students, teachers, and interested community members—what they think great learning looks like, what skills and abilities young people will need to lead happy and successful lives in a less knowable future, and the answers are in remarkable agreement: Deeper learning is better than shallow, student-centric learning is better than teacher-centric classrooms, questions and curiosity are more important than rote answers, understanding and wisdom are more important than mere knowledge.

The great transformation in which education is engaged in the first quarter of this 21st century is simply this: We are changing our focus from *what we teach* to *how we learn*. Forward-leaning schools are shifting, in the words of Bo Adams, from *teaching organizations* to *learning organizations*. Perhaps most of all, we are remembering that great learning is not the mere *transaction* of knowledge. Although that transaction is important, truly great learning centers on the *relationship* between learner and teacher, learner and co learners, learner and self, and learner and the experience of learning.

That leaves us with the critical and unanswered question of *how* education will make this enormous leap in such a short period of time, when we have been dramatically unsuccessful at making even a fraction of the leap over the last several decades. So far, well-intentioned solutions to pay teachers more, or fire teachers who are not good at their jobs, or build more schools, or lengthen the school day, or change the learning standards, or add more testing, or decrease testing have failed to move the needle very much. These solutions have failed because they are tweaks to a system that is in need of change, not by pruning, but at the roots.

How we transform education from the ground up, not a tweak or a reform, not for a few schools and a few students, but at scale, is the subject of this book. The problem is not that we lack the knowledge; we have examples all over the country and around the world of learning environments that offer a profoundly deeper, richer, better learning experience to their students. The problem is that we have failed to bring those solutions to scale. Every discussion about how to change education, based soundly on history and experience, grinds up against an enormous rock of *systemic inertia*. This rock is very real, very large, and has proven impossible to move very far from where it took root more than 100 years ago, despite the pull of necessity and the push of smart and well-meaning people.

> *Every discussion about how to change education, based soundly on history and experience, grinds up against an enormous rock of systemic inertia.*

Overcoming Inertia

Many, if not most, educators, parents, students, elected officials, and community stakeholders have given up, their heads sore or bloody from banging time and time again against this seemingly immovable rock. A growing number of families have found their way around the rock, or they are among the lucky who, because of personal or local economic and political conditions, have never been trapped by the rock. But moving the rock at scale, in a way that benefits the vast majority of students across widely diverse social and economic chasms, has been a Sisyphean myth. And yet, similar to the revolutions of farming, industry, and computing, it is utterly inevitable that the rock *will* move and that dramatic movement *will* take place in the very near future.

Simple physics tells us that a body at rest stays at rest until a force moves it. The big rock of K–12 education has tremendous mass, which means it sits firmly rooted with equally tremendous inertia. It will move only with the application of forces that are greater than the inertia that holds it in place. For decades, people of goodwill and sincere intent have prodded the system, looking for that adjustment in the design of school styles that would improve student outcomes. For decades, contrarian forces with which we are all familiar—the political left and right, government state houses, corporate and labor interests and those who savagely oppose those interests, funding and budgets that move from here to there and back again, research and studies that first say this program and then that one is *the* answer—have pushed on the rock in opposing directions with little net effect. The result is that education has grown more deeply resistant to real change than almost any social institution in the last century.

And yet, the rock *has* started to move, and unlike the familiar pendulum swings of education in the past, the new vector is irreversible. We have arrived at a major inflection point where the curve of global economic, social, environmental, and technological change is rising so steeply that fundamental alterations in our education system are inevitable. But that movement is still too slow and it is terribly uneven. Students with fewer societal supports and access to resources continue to be far less likely to participate in the leading edge of these changes, which means they are left farther behind as the leading edge accelerates.

What if we could move the static rock of education much more quickly? What if we found that we had a relatively small number of really huge "levers" that, if pressed firmly and synergistically, would actually move the rock in a dramatic fashion? Most important, what if those levers *Most important, what if those levers needed absolutely no resources or permission from the opposing political, economic, and social interests that have so successfully battled to keep the rock right where it sits for so long?* needed absolutely no resources or permission from the opposing political, economic, and social interests that have so successfully battled to keep the rock right where it sits for so long? And what if those levers already exist today, needing nothing more than *our* collective will to firmly grab hold and press hard?

This book is about those levers. Over the last several years I have visited more than 125 schools and districts around the country and interacted with well over 10,000 educators. I am the lucky guy without a job that keeps me tied to one school all day, so I get to read, observe, listen, imagine, synthesize, and dream. I put together input from that work, and then I reached out to about 80 other educational stakeholders: thought leaders, teachers, district administrators, researchers, and students. Most of the adults I have interviewed for this book share two other very important attributes: They all attended school themselves in the past, and many are parents or grandparents of children who will either thrive in a system tuned to their needs . . . or just muddle along with what many schools provide today.

I distilled what I heard from all of these stakeholders, and each major theme comprises a chapter of this book. Some of these levers have been lying nearly dormant for years or decades, ready for an explosive resurrection when the time was right. Some have been percolating at schools around the country and around the world, needing only the right conditions to move from isolated brushfires of innovation to successful use on a massive scale. Still others were born in just the last few years as new technologies intersect with this singular moment of enormous need and dramatic opportunity.

In addition to the key thesis that these levers must not require permission or empowerment from the forces that create systemic inertia, I set the following boundary conditions when deciding what levers to focus on:

- They align with the best interests of our students, even when those interests conflict with the interests of other powerful stakeholders.
- Many educators, parents, and students *want* these levers to be pressed.
- Each addresses a specific obstacle that has frustrated education reformers for years or decades and either breaks that obstacle or allows us to go around it in the very near future, with little or no increase in expense.
- All are completely possible today; in fact, they are already happening today in many schools. The only missing ingredient to bring them to scale is our collective will.

Where This Book Takes Us

In Chapter One I describe, based on the interviews I conducted for this book, a consensus view of what K–12 education will look like in 20 to 25 years. When taken together, it is a dramatically different picture than the institution we call "school" today and far beyond anything that most of us are thinking about. The consensus is that these dramatic changes to an institution that has remained largely unchanged for well over a century are inevitable. This is the future we have to plan for, and the trajectory we must initiate by pressing on big, audacious, nontraditional levers.

In Chapters Two through Eight I describe each of the seven levers that I have distilled from these interviews and work with schools since 2013:

Lever 1:   **Create the Demand for Better Schools.** Unlike just a decade ago, education is now subject to the market forces of supply and demand. All over the country, parents and families are voting with their feet and money. They are demanding a different approach to learning and seeking out nontraditional learning opportunities that meet those demands. Everyone in the community now has a direct pathway to influence schools toward a deeper learning experience.

Lever 2:   **Build School-Community Learning Laboratories.** Traditional schools are disconnected from their own communities and the powerful learning resources those communities can provide. We need to massively reconnect *school* and *world* in ways that deepen learning, better prepare students for life after school in the real world, and get broader community skin in the game. We need our students and teachers to "see the possible" in action in our own communities and with peers who can share their challenges and triumphs.

Lever 3:   **Encourage Open Access to Knowledge.** The rapid growth in the quality and availability of free, fully vetted curriculum, learning materials, and remarkable web-based knowledge sources will lead to the demise of expensive textbooks and other canned, outdated content delivery mechanisms. Schools can realize massive savings and redirect those scarce resources to much more critical needs while also providing learning materials that are better for our students and teachers.

Lever 4:   **Fix How We Measure Student Success and Admit Students to College.** Schools are afraid to adopt changes that might jeopardize their students' chances at college admissions. This fear among parents and students is one of the most powerful obstructions to school change. We are starting to see major cracks in this dam as colleges and high schools have begun to rethink what they value most, how to measure those values in individual students, and how to kill off the curse of test-driven education.

Lever 5:   **Teach the Teachers What They Really Need to Know.** Most postsecondary education schools are still preparing young teachers for an industrial age learning model that is on the wane, not the rise. We need a rapid, widespread, collaborative national overhaul of the teacher education program, led by courageous future-focused educators from research universities, teaching colleges, and the end users in K–12 schools.

Lever 6:   **Connect, Flow, and Rethink "School."** One set of levers for school change is being forged right now: a new universal set of pathways for creating and sharing information in the age of true digital transformation. Rapidly evolving virtual technologies will allow and force us to restructure learning . . . if educators help lead the way through our knowledge of how great learning actually occurs.

Lever 7:   **Lead Change from Where You Are.** Few educators have ever received training in the skills of management and organizational leadership that promote dynamic innovation in many of our leading companies . . . but are nearly absent in schools. Teachers and administrators need universal access to modern leadership skills that embrace, rather than stymie, change and innovation.

At the end of each of these chapters I suggest ways that each of us—parents, students, teachers, administrators, philanthropists, members of the university and business communities—can collectively turn the pioneering work of others into school transformation at scale. Some of the suggestions are for people and schools that are just starting to imagine such a transformation; others are for those who are more advanced. Some of these "challenges" may sound outlandish, impossible, or just plain dreamy . . . which is exactly what we need. But the fact is that almost all of these suggestions are based on what is *already working* today in schools and communities just like yours.

In Chapter Nine I lay out additional concrete, achievable actions that each of us can take to lend our weight to these levers, sorted by the hat you wear: teacher, student, administrator, parent, businessperson, and more. Now, I am not naive in thinking that these changes will explode across the system of K–12 education all at once; ecosystems do not adjust overnight. New species don't just pop up with all the right parts in all the right places; they evolve. What *you* do, the pieces that *you* tackle, the problems *you* solve, and the levers *you* press on *will* cumulatively change the system at scale. By each pressing somewhere, we collectively apply forces that actually move the rock. Not to completely give away my age and influences, but I believe it was the not-so-famous Wavy Gravy, who on the morning of the second day of the Woodstock Festival, looked out from the stage and shouted to the cold sea of people, grass, and mud: "It's about all of us, man; we're all helping each other!"

Finally, in a short Chapter Ten, I conclude with some big-picture takeaways and thoughts on the trajectory of schools that hope to intersect the inevitable future

> *What you do, the pieces that you tackle, the problems you solve, and the levers you press on will cumulatively change the system at scale.*

of education. And, at the end, I list organizations and resources cited by chapter (with hot links in the e-version of the book) so you have a great list to start connecting with others who have already pioneered pathways on all seven of the big levers of school transformation.

Resources for This Book

In addition to formal interviews and the distillation of hundreds or thousands of informal conversations with educators, I also had access to several other rich veins of unpublished collective thinking about these levers. John Gulla is the executive director of the EE Ford Foundation, a family philanthropic organization that supports independent high schools. John has freely shared with me his thoughts from visiting more than 200 schools around the country that are trying, in myriad ways, to reinvent elements of learning. I also was granted access to a study commissioned by The Peddie School, a day-boarding school in New Jersey that gathered insight from about 30 national thought leaders from inside and outside of education on the challenges that public and private schools face in the next two decades.

A rich resource that stretched my own ability to map the ground of education today and in the future was the research done in 2014–2015 by my colleague Julie Wilson, founder and executive director of the Institute for the Future of Learning. Julie was contracted by the Woodrow Wilson Foundation to gather insight into major trends, obstacles, and opportunities in K–12 education. She conducted phone and lengthy written-response interviews with more than a dozen well-known education thought and action leaders. Julie and the foundation made the results of her work available to me, and you will see citations from her report in several of the succeeding chapters.

What We Will Not Cover

No book can cover the entire map of the challenges of K–12 education, and I won't try here. Many of these key elements of the education revolution are being addressed by other researchers and authors: testing, standards-based instruction, project-based learning, the history and evolution of what we now recognize as a rigid, "industrial" model of education, changes in technology, and more. I have cited a number of these people and authoritative sources throughout the book and encourage you to add them to your libraries and learning communities.

There is one enormous subject I am intentionally *not* going to address, but which is, without a shred of doubt, *the biggest obstacle* to real education transformation: poverty. I want to forcefully emphasize that none of the levers I propose in this book will magically solve the problems of poverty and the special needs of students and families who are underserved by our society as a whole. There is a pervasive, entrenched, and in fact deepening and widening gap between those who have the realistic potential to take advantage of the value of a great education and those for whom the deck is overwhelmingly and unfavorably stacked. This trend is particularly pervasive in the United States but is certainly present in many developed and developing countries. Paul Tough, in his book *Helping Children Succeed,* sums up the depth of the problem: "In 2013, the United States reached an educational milestone. For the first time, a majority of the country's public school students—51 percent of them, to be precise—fell below the federal government's threshold for being 'low income,'" writes Paul. "Helping poor kids succeed is now, by definition, the central mission of American public schools and, by extension, a central responsibility of the American public. It is a responsibility we are failing to meet."

Students, families, teachers, and entire communities of poverty face daily obstacles beyond the imagination of the rest of us: crime, hunger, shelter, social disconnection, and as Robert Putnam so thoroughly demonstrates in his must-read book *Our Kids,* radically diminished access to many of the most basic support networks that the rest of us take for granted. Families of students with profound special needs face equally daunting obstacles for which I can't promise any solution because that is not my area of understanding. Education under these conditions of inadequate basic supports is an enormous strain on students, families, and teachers, and additional strain caused by leading the charge of large-scale change is probably unrealistic for some of these communities, at least for now.

That does not mean that poor communities and disadvantaged students will all be left behind, that poor schools and students cannot take on these challenges along with those more well served. To the contrary, there are examples in every community, every day, of these remarkable successes, of the richness of learning that takes place through and with the people, pride, and depth that all communities possess. A number of stories in this book reflect schools and individuals that are making this leap despite overwhelming odds. In fact, as we will see in the next chapter, as we look to what is inevitable about the transformation of schools in the next 20 to 25 years, many of the localized physical, social, and economic constraints experienced by underserved students and families will begin to erode with the growth of a vastly more networked, connected universe of learners and learning supporters. But I believe that poverty, similar to climate change and social justice, is one of those profound challenges to be tackled and solved by a well-educated populace, not one that must be solved before we can enact a new vision of education. I wish it were not so.

The Goal Is Deeper Learning

If we are going to transform education away from an assembly line model that worked well for the industrial age, we have to decide what we are transforming *toward*—the *what* of great learning that I mentioned. Among teachers, parents, students, and members of the university and business communities—who all have enormous stakes in how our students are being prepared for the future—there is vastly more agreement than disagreement about what great learning looks like. Yet although teachers and students may be aligned with what great learning outcomes *are,* they have a much harder time picturing a *process of learning* that is not a mirror of the past. Too many schools are still based on "doing learning to learners," when what we need is a system in which the learning is done "by and with the learner."

I am going to use a simple phrase—*deeper learning*—to capture these attributes and goals. In describing how education must evolve, others use terms such as *21st century learning* or *transformational learning,* and the educational community has gradually learned what these terms, in general, mean. Over the last several years, it seems that we are increasingly coalescing around the term *deeper learning* to describe a post-traditional, postindustrial, post–assembly line system of education that captures the essence of how schools are changing. I want to at least minimally define that term, which will show up many times in this book.

In 2013 the Hewlett Foundation defined *deeper learning* as "an umbrella term for the skills and knowledge that students must possess to succeed in 21st century jobs and civic life. At its

Over the last several years, it seems that we are increasingly coalescing around the term deeper learning to describe a post-traditional, postindustrial, post–assembly line system of education that captures the essence of how schools are changing.

heart it is a set of competencies students must master in order to develop a keen understanding of academic content and apply their knowledge to problems in the classroom and on the job." The six core competencies (about which readers may find a much more detailed articulation by simple web searches of *deeper learning*) are

- Mastering core academic content
- Thinking critically and solving complex problems
- Working collaboratively
- Communicating effectively
- Learning how to learn
- Developing academic mind-sets

Educators, schools, districts, and their community partners add meat to these bones in many different ways, and those who subscribe to the overall thesis also generally agree that there is no single cookbook recipe that works for all. Students and schools vary enormously in their needs and so must their learning. Having said that, I think there is a relatively discreet list of ways that schools are subscribing to, and implementing, the core ideas and competencies of deeper learning:

- Organizing learning on large, cross-disciplinary themes and ideas, not a small number of separate subject areas
- Empowering students with the responsibility to take concrete ownership of their learning process, including the ability to make choices based on interests and passions
- Students and teachers engaging in creating, not just transferring and consuming, knowledge
- Greater flexibility in the structure of the school day, with fewer hard-wired time periods
- Finding learning opportunities for students and adults outside the classroom, in the surrounding community, and among globally connected networks
- Building robust, sustainable communities of interest-based learning beyond the physical boundaries of classroom and campus

- Stretching and breaking the paradigm of one teacher and a fixed group of students
- Assessment and progress of students based on demonstrated competency, not just the time spent in a classroom or performance on tests that measure short-term memory
- Matching of students and adults during the day and year based on dynamic drivers of mutual interest and the needs of the individual student
- Vastly greater distribution of leadership and decision-making authority that allows risk-taking

It is in broadening the depth and reach of schools and districts that value, nurture, allow, empower, and *expect* these themes to drive the learning experience that the levers in this book can play such critical roles.

A Couple of Other Points

At several points in the book I will write harshly about standardized tests. These tests are not fundamentally bad as some would suggest; asking students to take exams that measure their progress and knowledge is an important part of education. We have to be able to measure things to know if we are getting the outcomes that we want. What I and many others believe is killing education is the *overuse* and *misuse* of standardized tests, where their impact is vastly exaggerated and abused.

Similarly, standards help teachers determine what to teach and how to teach it effectively. People frequently ask me where I stand on the issue of the Common Core Standards; in our increasingly polarized society it is comforting to be able to pigeonhole someone as being in the "for" or "against" camp about something controversial. So, here is what I think about the Common Core: I think there are people of goodwill, and who have the best interest of students in mind, who fall at opposite ends of this question, but I am not one of them. I find that many schools that are trying to build a deeper learning experience for their students agree with me when I say this: If your school or district views the Common Core as a bar you are trying to reach, it will be difficult to create a true deeper learning experience. If, however, your school reads these standards carefully, and views the Common Core as a floor on which to build upwards, there is nothing to fear, and the standards can be a good starting point. I am pretty sure that every one of the schools that I cite in this book for leading the way in deeper learning experiences is also meeting Common Core Standards.

Finally, I have tried to write this book with a diverse audience in mind. I am sure that many readers will be professional educators, but I hope that many are not, so I have tried to keep the use of educational jargon to a minimum. I can't avoid the use of one word that will sound "jargony" to non-educators: *pedagogy*. There is just no other word to replace it; it is a good word! Don't be afraid; *pedagogy* just refers to methods of teaching or instruction. Teachers who lecture for 45 minutes, for example, are using a different pedagogy than teachers who help their students find problems and collaboratively solve them. The evolution from the model of learning that most of us adults experienced when we were in school to a deeper learning model starts with a change in pedagogy.

Let's Roll

I can't count the times over the last five years that I wished some smart marketing team had never suggested the slogan "Just Do It" to Nike, Inc. It is the perfect call to action for all of us who have a stake in great education. But who wants to risk a copyright lawsuit from one of the biggest companies on the planet? So, alternately, and with complete respect, I remind us of that morning in September 2001, after two planes had slammed into the World Trade Center and one into the Pentagon, that on a fourth plane, United Flight 93, passenger Todd Beamer courageously asked his seatmates, "Are you ready? OK. Let's roll." The first entry in *Wikipedia* under the topic "let's roll" says that it is a "colloquial catchphrase that has been used extensively as a command to move and start an activity, attack, mission, or project." Well, it is time to stop pushing the education rock back and forth, to stop inactive talk, to stop obsessing over the fine points of disagreement, and to stop pointing fingers of blame about why schools are failing to serve all of our students. This is *our* responsibility, *our* critical mission, not someone else's, and *we* can't shrug it off. It is time to roll.

Throughout this book I share examples of teachers, students, schools, parents, districts, and other community stakeholders who are already pressing hard on these levers of change. I could write a book 10 times as long with all of the examples I have uncovered, and I have only uncovered a

> *It is time to stop pushing the education rock back and forth, to stop inactive talk, to stop obsessing over the fine points of disagreement, and to stop pointing fingers of blame about why schools are failing to serve all of our students.*

fraction of the incredible transformation that is taking place in schools and communities across America, let alone the rest of the world. Is there a magic formula that will change schools overnight like Cinderella's pumpkin? No. Unfortunately change at scale will not be as fast or as equitable as we would like, but we *can* move from isolated successful pilots to scaled implementation when possible, and we have to do that *now*. If we continue to micro-focus on the value of one standardized test over another, the political correctness of a few sentences in a history text, the correct science sequence in high school, or the relative value of one math or literacy approach over the other, we will condemn at least another generation of students to spend their entire formative lifetimes in a system that is not preparing them for their futures as well as we can. That is just not morally acceptable.

With that, let's roll.

CHAPTER ONE

The Future of "School"

If you think in terms of a year, plant a seed; if in terms of 10 years, plant trees; if in terms of 100 years, teach the people.

Confucius

Albermarle County stretches across rural rolling hills from the red brick monuments of the University of Virginia to backwoods grade schools in some of the poorest corners of central Appalachia. One might look elsewhere for the changing fabric of education, unless one had heard of Pam Moran, the diminutive, insightful, fiery, passionate superintendent of Albermarle County Schools who has gained a well-deserved international reputation for breaking pretty much any boundary that stands in the way of great learning for her 13,000+ students. Pam, her supporting cast of educational leaders, and their students have been featured in articles, on television, and across educational social media as they rethink and rework the place we call "school." Their students gather in informal, somewhat noisy collaborative spaces that used to be hushed quiet by attentive librarians. Budding student musicians and robot-loving techies, who used to rush off campus after the last bell of the day, now hang out after-hours in the recording studios and the maker spaces, publishing their latest songs and building stuff out of odds and ends. Teachers are celebrated, not disciplined, for taking risks. One principal moved his desk into the middle of the school entry hall to make the point that his job is "in" the school, not behind a closed door.

Albermarle County does not have deep pockets, and many of their students come from underserved communities where education is poorly understood and often not supported in the traditional social fabrics of farm, town, and family. But Pam says that "what is emerging right now, what is coming out of work we have been doing over the last decade when budgets have been very tight, is a network of choices and opportunities that are not dependent on funding or direction from the government. We have been forced to figure out ways to encourage schools to adapt beyond-the-horizon opportunities for our students" relying largely on themselves. What sets Albermarle County schools apart from many other districts is that they have actually done it, not fearfully or cautiously or tentatively, but boldly and courageously.

Redesigning the School "Operating System"

The education-industrial community, the system that is hugely responsible for shaping the lives and opportunities for *your children,* spends billions of dollars every year and an endless flood of human capital in building, updating, and reforming the "hardware" and "software" of K–12 education. The problem is that we have virtually ignored the K–12 education "operating system," which has not had a substantial redesign since the middle of the 19th century. We will not fundamentally change education until we stop designing around an operating system that is 150 years old. *How* we change this operating system by finally getting around, over, or past the frictions that have kept it stuck is the problem we need to solve.

Whether you are a parent, an employer, or a classroom teacher, it is highly probable that you underestimate the magnitude of change coming to K–12 education. As I detailed in an article for the Transforming Teaching Project at the Harvard Graduate School of Education (Lichtman, 2015), the K–12 operating system includes not only physical campuses and teams of people but also the processes, standards, assumptions, and mind-sets that determine how schools have worked for at least 150 years. The current K–12 education operating system guides everything a school does: how we measure student progress; how we compartmentalize learning by subject; how we assign teachers to groups of students; our outdated daily and annual schedules; suffocating and ineffective professional development for our teachers; vast overuse of standardized testing; rigid, top-down decision making; prison-like physical campuses; and impermeable boundaries between schools and the communities they serve.

This system performed extraordinarily well when measured against the economic and social needs of the late-19th through mid-20th centuries when the alternatives for learning were limited largely to cloistered monasteries, ivy towers, and red one-room schoolhouses. Most educators and many students and parents, similar to those in Albermarle County, recognize that the system is critically flawed when matched against the outcomes we want for students in the 21st century. And yet most educators continue to design curriculum, instructional practices, assessment, schedules, training, physical campuses, support systems, and new digital technologies for a system that no longer meets current and future expectations. As Alan Daly, chair of the education department at the University of California, San Diego, told me "We are not thinking about education at a systems level. We think in narrowly defined parts and believe that if we can hone practice or solve a problem in one narrow area then all will be well, and this is just wrong. We have to intersect much more carefully and systematically among teachers, districts, colleges, student-users, and community stakeholders as co-thinkers, codesigners, and co-constructors of a better *system* of learning."

Where the Rock Is Going to Roll

So, let's ask the question: *What will "school" look like in 20 or 25 years?* Will the type of dramatic changes we see taking root in places such as Albermarle County schools over the last decade become the norm, or will they still be outliers? What is the inevitable future with which we must try to intersect? In work with John Gulla of the EE Ford Foundation in 2016, we reflected on the hundreds of schools, thousands of educators, and numerous education thought leaders with whom we have collectively crossed paths in the last five years and offered this general vision:

> Adult and student co-learners will seamlessly connect physically and virtually via multiple optional pathways in a web-like, global, socio-neural network to create and share wisdom and knowledge,

unrestricted by the bonds of time and space, unfettered by the boundaries of subject, classroom, and age, and learning skills and tackling timeless questions and profound problems that face us as individuals, as communities, and as a species. "Schools" will be critical portals into this web of practice, physical places where we gather as relationship-rich communities. These school portals will offer spaces to interact in traditional face-to-face settings as well as providing easy access to individual and group virtual reality devices with which learners in one physical location can form deep, authentic relationships with multiple co-learners in any other spot on the globe. Adult and student co-learners will share insights, experiences, and data, generating artifacts of ideas and actual physical objects that will "print" anytime, anywhere. The sum of human knowledge and, increasingly, nuance will be accessible to anyone on the globe with an Internet-connected device, in real time by posing questions in a common language without the need to query, program, or understand how a computer thinks differently from how a human thinks. Adults and children of all ages will be teamed according to their respective unique talents, aptitudes, interests, and passions, progressing at differentiated rates through a series of increasingly complex challenges as they grow in understanding and ability. School will not be an event that occupies our lives for 10 months a year for 12 or 14 or 20 years in our youth. We will all be connected to "school" throughout our childhood and adult lives, diving in when we need, to find what we need, for as long as we need.

If this future is inevitable, what will happen to the big pieces of the education operating system: classrooms and buildings, the teachers, unions, textbook companies, district offices, and administrators? What will happen to the architects who design campuses, bus drivers who pick up our kids in the morning, and the single moms who need somewhere for their children to go during the work day? What will happen to our 150-year social commitment to public education that is open and available to all? Will these all completely disappear in 20 years? Hopefully not; the richest elements of truly transformational learning are relational, not transactional, and these relationships can develop only when a diverse group of students and adults spend a great deal of time together.

But there will be dramatic changes way beyond what many educators conceive today. Many of these changes are already taking shape. Families have much greater choice about how and where their children learn than just a decade ago. That curve, along with other demographic, economic, techno- logical, and social trends, is only growing steeper and, in fact, may be leading to a step-function leap unlike anything the system of education has seen since the invention of the printing press. Twenty years from now there will have been a series of tectonic shifts of people, money, and other resources away from mainstream traditional public and private schools into alternative learning systems that are fundamentally different from the dominant models today. Those shifts will have disrupted the lives of many within the extended system of education. Some people and schools will adapt; others will probably not. That is the nature of real evolution: some species and individuals thrive while others die out.

Twenty years from now there will have been a series of tectonic shifts of people, money, and other resources away from mainstream traditional public and private schools into alternative learning systems that are fundamentally different from the dominant models today.

How Will the Learning Experience Change?

Students, teachers, and sources of knowledge will be hyper-connected via a variety of virtual pathways, most of which have not been invented yet. Every student and teacher will have Internet-enabled devices that are either free or extremely cheap. There will be no hard textbooks. Students and teachers will access content from universal libraries of digital curriculum that are open source, fully accredited, and free.

Rather than treating all students as part of an averaged group, the primary academic focus will be on how well a student can explore and learn along a "lane" tailored specifically to each individual. The sorting of students that now takes place largely along lines of test-based scholastic aptitude will broaden to include a combination of aptitude, interest, learning style, and social-emotional abilities. There will be few, if any, subject boundaries; learning will take place across broad interdisciplinary themes that combine real-world problems and direct experience. K–12 and post-secondary learning systems will have adopted a vastly greater emphasis on social and emotional awareness that helps create a balanced life for students and teachers.

How Will Schools Function Differently?

Physical schools will still exist, but students and adults will spend much more time in a diverse ecosystem of physical and virtual communities and less in isolated classrooms. Schools will have developed powerful student and adult partnerships with colleges, universities, companies, incubators, laboratories, and nonprofit nodes in this greater learning ecosystem. Daily schedules will have many fewer, if any, boundaries, and 10-week summer vacations will have largely disappeared.

The static teacher-student ratio, one teacher in a room with a given number of students for a fixed period of time, will become vastly more fluid. All teachers will *not* be essentially similar cogs on a wheel with the same skill sets or expectations. Schools will have a mixture of master teachers, assistants, coaches, tutors, and mentors, connecting with students physically and virtually. Frequent, ongoing professional development and the desire on the part of teachers to continue to learn and grow throughout their careers will be absolute job requirements.

Our teacher-mentor-coaches will mostly be members of the millennial generation, digital natives, used to a vastly more flexible lifestyle than the now-retiring population of baby boomers. School leaders will also mostly be millennials, less tied to tradition and more willing to take risks, unless schools continue to make the deadly mistake of filtering out job applicants with those critical qualities. In order to keep pace with the rate of change, successful schools will have adopted flat, distributed management systems that require decisions to be made across the organization, which means that educators will be valued for their strength of creativity, teamwork, and comfort in dynamic settings.

How Will Our Mission Shift?

The learning experience will focus on the needs of individual students in ways that our largely cookie-cutter classrooms, curriculum, and assessment protocols fail to do today. Educators and parents will tackle ongoing new issues of physical and virtual safety as the boundaries of learning breach the walls of classroom and campus. College and career-readiness goals will shift as colleges wrestle with massive dissonance about their own missions and as many of the jobs that our students will encounter don't even exist today. Colleges will have changed their admissions criteria away from the failed focus on standardized tests, allowing secondary schools to offer a much wider range of courses and experiences tailored to each student. Performance or badge-based job apprenticeship opportunities will be intimately wrapped together with classroom-like education as the boundaries of what students learn and how that learning might be applied are dramatically more "smeared" than they are today.

As schools seek to find a powerful or even unique set of conditions that will offer truly differentiated value to customer families, community stakeholders will be involved in virtually every decision that affects learning, including strategy and implementation of evolving practices. Schools will have richer, real-time customer-feedback systems in order to align the desires and needs of individual students and families with their school experience.

Why Is This Future Inevitable?

Is this really what learning will look, feel, and act like in just 20 years? Might this crystal ball be off in the time line and scope? Sure, but not by much. Lacking a global social, economic, political, or environmental meltdown, this transformation in education won't take 50 or 100 years, and something very much like this future state is inevitable. Those of us who work in schools know that school years are sort of like dog years: Five years can pass on the world calendar in almost the

... nearly all of the elements of this future are already percolating in place or incubating in our imagination, design studios, and schools today.

blink of a school's eye. And, as we will see in this book, nearly all of the elements of this future are already percolating in place or incubating in our imagination, design studios, and schools today.

These dramatic changes to our educational system are inevitable for four reasons:

- First, **because we must.** The world that our young people will engage over their lifetimes is already very different from that of former generations, and it will likely become even more different as the rate of change accelerates. Although there will always be a timeless set of knowledge that helps in this preparation, students graduating and hoping to find a job in the developed world need skills that help them navigate a future that is increasingly VUCA (volatile, uncertain, complex, and ambiguous). The tectonic shifts from the industrial to the information age require our students to be able to think, not just know. If education does not prepare our students to deal with this future, then the value proposition of an equitable, broad, rich, liberal arts education, let alone one focused on passing standardized fill-in-the-bubble tests, becomes decreasingly attractive to value-conscious consumers.

- Second, **because we want to.** I, and many others, some of whom you will hear from in this book, have asked thousands of educators, parents, students, and community stakeholders what they want education to look like today and in the future, and there is tremendous agreement. We want a system that is more equally balanced between academic achievement and the development of noncognitive skills that prepare students to lead happy, healthy, and successful lives. If our traditional schools do not offer the community of consumer stakeholders what they want, they will find it somewhere else.

- Third, **because we know better.** Past evidence on how children learn has reflected the work of sociologists, psychologists, and educational researchers. These are now joined by cognitive neuro-scientists armed with brain-mapping technology that proves how learning takes place at its most foundational levels. We can see how engagement takes place within the brain and can connect that engagement to better levels of cognitive development through the processes of deeper learning.
- Fourth, **because we can.** Technology is never the *driver* of trans-formation, but it is always a critical *enabler.* Recall this simple fact: The Pony Express was the best communication technology across long distances in North America in 1860. By 1920, just 60 years later, roughly a third of American homes had a telephone. Similar to the rise of technologies that fueled the agrarian, industrial, and information revolutions, holographic and virtual technologies are already forming the basis of a global socio-neural network with the capacity for deep, authentic, relationship-based learning that does not require the traditional school operating system. Just as we are finding ways to treat cancer patients based on their individual genetics, data-mining technologies and artificial intelligence will increasingly enable us to know what does and does not work better in terms of learning for each individual student.

There is no cookie-cutter model for schools in the future. What John Gulla calls "the urgent insecurity of a frightening world" does not affect all families in the same way, and that will be increasingly reflected in a range of educational approaches that meet the needs of individual students. A broad spectrum of learning opportunities already exists for many families and, with a global economy and social structure that has fundamentally mutated from producer-driven to consumer-driven, there is every reason to believe that the differentiation of these opportunities will only continue to increase.

If these visions of the future, about which there is great concern and tremendous enthusiasm, are even *somewhat* correct, then *how* we make the transition is where we must focus our attention. There are two end-member pathways for how these changes will take place. In the first, we learn from our knowledge of history and our mistakes of the past. We stop banging our collective heads against unyielding walls of special interests that kill innovation, that keep the rock of education rooted in place. All of the community stakeholders who see how powerful learning can become when we break the chains of an outdated system press these levers that are available to us. We just do it.

The alternative is to let the passage of history and the inevitable evolution of human social systems fill the gap between need and capacity, in which case our current system of education will not evolve and morph into the future; it will dissolve piecemeal or blow up quickly, a mutation that will be vastly more disruptive than if we choose the first path. I emphasize again: The march of human history has *never* withstood the dissonance between what we need and our ability to achieve it. These changes are *going* to happen; the only question now is *how*. We each have a choice. We can choose to ignore the signs, or *we* get to make *how* happen. As you will see in the rest of this book, there are people across every category of the school-community spectrum who are making these changes a reality today. This future is actually *not* far-fetched or improbable; it is already taking shape in towns and cities and schools just like yours.

CHAPTER TWO

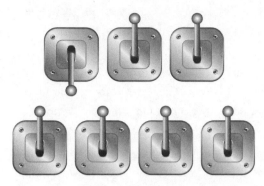

Lever #1
Create the Demand for Better Schools

Power concedes nothing without a demand. It never did and it never will.
Frederick Douglass

A lever without a place to slot into the system is just a club hanging in the air.
Larry Singer

Forty years ago, Cajon Valley Union School District was a dusty backwater in the sage-covered granite hills east of San Diego. Like much of America, land values closer to the downtown urban core soared in the previous few decades. Bright new middle- and upper-middle-class neighborhoods sprang up in those hills and valleys, tile-roofed homes on neat cul-de-sacs bought by two-income parents willing to put up with long commutes on ever-more crowded freeways. Along with those houses came newer schools with modern buildings and shiny playgrounds. Once homogeneously middle and working class, now Cajon Valley has pockets of wealthier and poorer families. District-wide school choice followed, and families living near Rios Elementary School voted with their cars and feet to send their kids to the newer schools, which gradually took on the reputation of being "better" through the reinforcing feedback loop of higher incomes and higher test scores. Enrollment at Rios dropped; at a school built to house 700 students, by the Spring of 2016 there were just 250.

Superintendent David Miyashiro and principal Maria Kehoe hired a marketing consultant to re-brand Rios as a computer science magnet to help rebuild enrollment. "Simply," says Maria, "we have a great, unique product here but people don't know about it." I attended an afternoon event, wandering the hallways among crowds of proud parents and grandparents, celebrating in wonder the creative robots and fanciful, simple machines that had excited their students so much all year. Maria had advertised the event across the community, hanging notices in small stores, restaurants, and taco shops. Maria says that "one of the new roles of a successful principal is as 'brand champion.' We are going to capture the attention of parents who value what we value, both here in the neighborhood and those who might be driving past us on their commute." Maria surveyed parents who had opted to move to another school in the last few years and found that many left simply because Rios lost funding for early drop-off care in the morning. Maria is going to shift resources around to get that back, and then she is going to work like heck to get the message out that Rios is meeting the needs of the community's working families. It is all paying off; by the winter of 2017, enrollment at Rios was up by 90 students.

Rios Elementary is the face of changing public education in America. The school is a community asset but only as long as they can convince families next door and across town that what they offer is somehow unique or better for the children. Like it or not, K–12 education is now a dynamic, open, fluid marketplace that responds to the powerful laws of supply and demand.

As a former geologist, I see change in the world around us, from tiny and inconsequential to life-changing and catastrophic, as the passage of time intersecting with natural and human forces. A hiker on a still morning in the high canyons might hear a single rock ping down the cliffs somewhere far above, knowing it is probably just a pebble dislodged by a ground squirrel or a rabbit or perhaps the early spring thaw. One lonely rock may be just that, or it may be the forerunner of a slide that grows with the inexorable pull of gravity and the growing mass of many, many rocks moving downhill with gathering speed that smashes trees and brush and anything else in its way. That is the nature of rocks when they roll. Sometimes it is a pretty echo in the morning; sometimes it wipes out the valley. This chapter is about how we all can help ensure that schools choose elegant change and are not swept away in a chaotic upheaval.

Like gravity, the market forces of supply and demand are universal and inevitable. The failed 20th century experiments of large-scale social and economic communism laid to rest any illusion that markets do not respond powerfully to such forces. The influence of supply and demand has grown even more powerful in a world flattened by widespread access to information, communication, transportation, and the increasingly unbounded global flows of knowledge and capital. In the first quintile of the 21st century we have undergone a fundamental and nearly universal reversal in the relationship between large suppliers and many consumers. For centuries large producers and suppliers have told consumers, in effect, "here is what we have to sell; you will buy it." Across nearly every sector, consumers now say, "here is what I want to buy; sell it to me." We self-select individual songs on iTunes instead of buying a CD of songs chosen for us by a large music company; we choose what stocks to own on eTrade rather than blindly trust the recommendations of a big bank; we search for merchandise and deals on Amazon or eBay rather than just buying what is on the shelf at Sears. Although sometimes education is glacially slow to change, this fundamental shift is rattling the rocks high in the canyons, and those who are not already heeding the warning of those crashing rocks will soon be swept aside.

The coming landslide reflects the cumulative change in demand by education consumers, which includes everyone reading this book. Primary and secondary education in the developed world, and in much of the developing world as well, has largely been a monopoly of the state for the last 150 years. These monopolies have positively affected many citizens, albeit unequally, allowing at least some degree of upward mobility based on talent, hard work, and social support. John Gulla of the EE Ford Foundation describes a relatively simple marketplace of American education through the first years of the 21st century. "Less than a generation ago, there were essentially three types of school, with three distinct cost-value points," says John. "There were public schools, paid for, largely, through non-optional property taxes, that served 85–90% of families; there were faith-based, mostly parochial schools that were subsidized by religious organizations; and there were private schools that, on average cost twice as much as the faith-based schools to attend. Other than a very small number of home-schooled children, that pretty much described the marketplace of American K–12 education." Until very recently, the supply of education was restricted, so demands for change had little impact.

No more. The education oligarchy is in a period of mutation that started with the charter school movement in the 1990s, and now, with the rapid evolution of information technologies, is quickly becoming a full-fledged landslide. At the lower-cost end, families may decide to send their children to choice, magnet, or charter schools that may require a fee for bus transportation or special classroom enrichment programs. Increasingly, when public schools have cut back on arts, athletics, or interest-based electives, and for families that can afford it, students attend optional fee-based after-school and summer enrichment programs or take classes online through a complex marketplace of providers that did not even exist 15 years ago. At the higher cost end, there is a dizzying array of online schools, hybrid schools, gap-year programs, and alternative learning experiences that challenge the cost-value proposition of traditional private schools.

Up until the last decade, most school leaders did not have to worry about their school's value proposition as seen through the eyes of consumers. Most consumers had little or no choice about where to send their children for education; attendance at neighborhood schools was the norm. That is increasingly not the case, and public school leaders find themselves fighting to attract and retain students in much the same way that private schools have for decades. In the past, the supply of education was essentially a constant, and the demands of consumers were largely irrelevant. Today, the supply side of the equation is exploding in terms of differentiated types of "school" driven by changing consumer demands. What does this mean for changing our schools at scale? It means that parents, students, and proponents of educational transformation now have an enormous lever that did not even exist a decade or so ago. *We* can change schools by, simply, demanding that they change.

Creating Demand at the National Level

After more than 20 years working in the realm of education public policy in Washington, DC, Ken Kay says he came to the realization that top-down policy is not a great lever for changing schools. Ken, founder of EdLeader21, a consortium of several hundred change-oriented public and private schools and districts around the country, says that for decades he had a strong bias that top-down directives were a driver of transformation. "I have been completely disabused of that," says Ken. "Transformation is going to be led by districts and schools from the bottom up. We are coming up on a change in the demand curve. Districts that are shifting practice are doing so *in spite* of public policy, not because of it. When we get a dozen or two districts in a state moving toward real transformation we will start to see a softening of the intransigence in state houses."

Most state and federal bureaucracies are just too big, too unwieldy, too influenced by interests that do not reflect what is best for students, and too far from the classroom to be effective drivers of deeper learning. Ken told me about an EdLeader21 meeting with a large group of superintendents in Missouri, "some of whom really recognize the need to transform their districts. One said 'we need to get the governor and legislature on board.' I asked 'does anyone in here actually think state policy is going to get things right in education in the next decade?' No one raised [his or her] hand. When someone says the problem is the governor or the legislature, it sounds like you can't do anything without their permission. The opposite is true; the only way we actually change is when schools change without explicit permission."

When someone says the problem is the governor or the legislature, it sounds like you can't do anything without their permission. The opposite is true; the only way we actually change is when schools change without explicit permission.

Famous people with household names and anonymous deep-pocket investors are starting to help create demand for real change with huge budgets, national marketing campaigns, and highly targeted projects that they hope will fundamentally shift the conversation about education in America away from the now decades-long demand for higher test scores. Investors such as Facebook mogul Mark Zuckerberg and many others have cumulatively put hundreds of millions of dollars into new models of public and private schools, some with the expectation of financial return and others with the simple hope of shaking the system to its core. Nonprofits such as Education Reimagined in The Convergence Center for Policy Resolution in Washington, DC, and Transcend Education based in

New York have gathered large groups of leading education stakeholders together to design and launch national clearinghouses and collaborative networks for educators to build and share common language and practices in deeper learning education.

One of the most commonly cited and most accessible sparks for dramatic school change is the movie *Most Likely to Succeed,* a documentary focused on High Tech High Schools in California. Funded by veteran venture-capitalist-turned-philanthropist Ted Dintersmith, and shaped by Harvard professor, author, and education thought leader Tony Wagner, the movie has been screened by schools and districts in every state. Many of the people I interviewed for this book said that the movie, along with others such as *Race to Nowhere* and *Beyond Measure* and accompanying books, had created that critical "ah-ha" moment, when diverse groups of teachers, parents, and others from across the community realized that the education their students have been receiving is in dramatic need of resuscitation and that remedies are already in place, if they only have the courage to look.

Perhaps the most audacious national-level mark was set by philanthropist and long-time advocate of equitable education, Laurene Powell Jobs, when she created the national XQ America Challenge, offering $50 million in start-up funding for game-changing ideas about how to operate high schools, supporting the challenge with a sustained television and social media marketing blitz unlike anything we have ever seen in American education. The response was so deep and wide, and the number of outstanding proposals so large, that Laurene doubled her commitment to $100 million. In an update in January 2017, CEO of XQ Russlynn Ali told me that they were "blown away by the authentic faith in public education when we empower people to think about and design schools as hubs of their communities. As we toured the country, thousands of people, many hobbled by poverty and the achievement gap in their students, came out to tell us their stories and their dreams." The challenge created a forum for more than 45,000 people to think about a better form of education and, according to Russlynn, several months after the awards were announced, "more than 125 teams that did *not* win are still engaged in the process. We see ideas for true breakthroughs in the use of time, space, technology, and community resources in these ideas. And they are coming not just from educators, but from such a diverse group of education supporters; there were 59 different occupations represented in the profiles of team members. We see the Challenge as one rung on a ladder of change, ownership, and agency about what happens in these communities at their own schools."

Carlos Moreno, of the Big Picture Learning network of schools says that large, well-funded, national-scale projects such as these are effective ignition points for change because school leaders can look at schools in a familiar, nearby setting. "We had about 50 school leaders from Arkansas, Florida, and Tennessee come visit one of our BPL schools in Nashville," says Carlos. "It looks a lot more familiar to them than taking them to a school up in New England or on the West Coast. Once educators see what is possible they realize it is very much within their own reach as well."

Although big dollars and famous names help create demand and buzz, large groups of individual parents and students can have a major impact on education policy using nothing more than the power of choice, the influence of connected social media, and the 24-hour news cycle. The Opt Out movement grew out of parental distaste with school districts that have become so overly focused on test results that some students spend as much as 30% of the school year just preparing for standardized exams. Most states allow parents to give permission for their students to opt out of taking these exams, despite often intense pressure, particularly in high-performing schools, where results reflect well on the district. Long-time progressive education leader Chris Thinnes says that, although some mass movements are futile, "Opt Out has already been successful in gar-nering huge amounts of public attention, and in places like Seattle, it has led to real changes in how school works, because a fairly large number of teachers, parents, and students just said 'no' to a system that does not align with their idea of good education."

Creating Demand at the School Level

Although nothing attracts mass attention like a movie release, a $100 mil-lion pot of gold, a national advertising campaign, or a protest line with moms and little kids on the evening news, the real shift in demand comes at the grassroots level when schools listen to the changing wishes and needs of individual families. Superintendent Pam Moran, the legendary leader of the Albermarle County District in Virginia, points to how her district has simultaneously pushed the demand levers for deeper learning on three fronts: with teachers, students, and parents. They held public showings of "Most Likely to Succeed" to get community support for ideas such as space redesign, STEM laboratories, and student-led projects, which led to excitement among principals and teachers. As stories and examples of highly engaged students and rising outcomes percolate around the district, Pam says, "teachers see it and want to re-create the same levels of engagement in their own classes and their own schools. We support teachers to see themselves as inventors, learners, and creators." They encourage teachers to participate and share their experiments on social media, which Pam says acts as "a kind of viral influence that spreads through and outside the district. We plant the seeds and give them resources, and the teachers at some other school, or after a few years, don't even know where the ideas sprouted from."

According to Pam, as word spread around Albermarle County, the demand from students for deeper learning exploded. "When we turned our library into a Learning Commons we went from 400 student visits a year to 70,000 visits per year. In our small music studio students are writing, recording, producing, and selling their music on iTunes. We have a very diverse demographic and every kind of student is comfortable in that studio. We are cutting across the traditional social lines of a school. Rather than imposing change, we see it spread more like a social virus of inventive ideas that have a common thread of student agency. The students will wade through all kinds of traditional content in their courses, and do much better in those courses, if they see how it helps them do something they actually find relevant."

Vista Unified School District in Southern California, winners of one of the coveted XQ America Challenge awards, started to build demand for deeper learning with the lowest-performing school and the most underserved student population in the district with the courageous thesis that if the changes could succeed there, other schools and their stakeholders would follow. In one year, they converted a low-performing middle school with declining enrollment into the Vista Innovation and Design

Academy, with a focused mission on design thinking, innovation, and student-centered learning. Superintendent Devin Vodicka says that "the rest of the district is able to see what principal Eric Chagala and his team are doing at VIDA and say 'there is nothing magical about that; we can do that, too.' The transformation at VIDA has been dramatic. I can't create that same path for all of our schools, but I can give them the same opportunity to change and promise to support them in whatever path they derive that is going to be best for their students. To see VIDA move so dramatically created a real impact on the whole community." It is not a coincidence that, with this kind of incubator thinking and support, Vista Unified was one of the winners of the XQ America challenge. Devin recites an imperative from visionary Margaret Wheatley that leaders are required to ask themselves "what is possible? Our job is just to bring people together to do what most think is impossible," says Devin.

We see similar results as leaders all over the country create opportunities for teachers and parents to see, touch, and feel a deeper learning environment. At Elizabeth Forward Middle School in Elizabeth, Pennsylvania, assistant superintendent Todd Keruksin says that it all boils down to leadership, the willingness to try something new. "We have found that the only way to do this," says Todd, "is for superintendents and assistant superintendents to get out of the office, to spend a lot of time and focus with principals and other site leaders, to 'make them feel awkward.' If you don't learn this yourself, you can't talk to your teachers and parents about where education is going and the opportunities we can provide in the future. Once they experience it themselves, many get enthusiastic and then the transformation starts in their own schools."

Some people think that these big changes can only take place in charter or private schools, and that is just not true. Regan Drew and John Marshall are cofounders of Riverpoint Academy, a non-charter public school in the Mead School District near Spokane, Washington. The rapidly growing academy incorporates many elements of a deeper learning model: longer class periods, student-led project work, and rich interactions with the community. John says that understanding and acceptance across the community of what they are doing at the academy started slowly, but it is accelerating. "At first, many other teachers in the district felt that teachers at the Academy were 'different from us,' but now we are collaborating with peers at other schools on a number of ideas and projects. It's informal, but in large organizations, that is just how things get done. It doesn't mean we are out proselytizing; we just find people through mutual interests and things start to change."

Regan told me that early in the Riverpoint roll-out there was a lot of tension among other teachers in the district. "They were all working hard and doing their best and all of a sudden we are creating a new model and the first reaction among the other educators is 'we aren't doing something well.' They took it personally; there was fear that what they had done in the past was being rejected. When we got them to look at what we are doing, and built those relationships, the attitude changed pretty quickly to 'this is great!'" Of course, there are structural barriers at other schools within the district that limit what other teachers can do, even when they get excited. "John and I co-teach the entire day with a cohort of 40 students and we have them all day long," says Regan. "Other teachers are constrained by short periods based on subject matter. They can't really adopt much of what we are doing given their structures, but they now see that the traditional structures are what is standing in the way of a better learning environment for the kids."

Creating Demand in the Community

As schools are forced to become more proactive with current and prospective families in order to attract and retain students, they are learning to listen to, work with, and communicate better with community stakeholders . . . particularly parents.

As I explained in *#EdJourney*, every school and district has a value proposition based on the choices that school leaders and parents are now free to make. School leaders are learning how to develop and share a clear value proposition with their community of stakeholders or

School leaders are learning how to develop and share a clear value proposition with their community of stakeholders or risk losing students to other schools where the value more closely and clearly matches that of the families they serve.

risk losing students to other schools where the value more closely and clearly matches that of the families they serve. Simply, schools are learning how to market themselves. Although some educational purists cringe at that idea, I push back on two fronts. First, that is just the way the world works now. And second, it is a good thing for schools to decide how they will be great, because when they do, more kids win.

Pam Moran at Albermarle County says that they have been highly intentional about reaching out with examples of the transformed learning environment to parents, many of whom have been among the most disengaged with their children's education. "We have targeted low-performing students, with parents who we could never get to even return our phone calls," says Pam. "Many of these kids are now highly engaged; we see vastly fewer discipline problems and a huge acceleration in performance even when compared to Advanced Placement students. The parents see that and are now coming to back-to-school night early in the year and saying 'my kid never wanted to even *talk* about school and now they want to go to school every day.' Parents are asking 'how can I get my kid into that? How can I make sure my student gets more of *that* kind of experience next year?' Parents wouldn't *let* us stop these programs now." Similarly, as Vista Unified watches the growth and evolution of VIDA, Devin Vodicka says that the demand curve has completely reversed from a school that was losing students to one in high demand. "Parents with one kid at VIDA and one at another school now ask, 'Why don't I see that same kind of excitement about school at the other site?'"

Unfortunately, some families are better able to make choices or to even know about their options than others; choice is rarely equitable. Eric Juli at Design Lab Early College High School in Cleveland, a non-charter public school that is attracting low-income students from all over urban Cleveland, says that parents have to actually *see* what takes place at the school, and this is very hard with poor families who often don't have a car or even money for bus fare. "This year we invited prospective families to a 'maker night' where we showcased our new maker spaces and gave the parents a little window into what our students are doing. Ninety percent of those who came to these nights signed up to attend our school, while only about 5% of parents who inquired about the school but who did not actually visit us ended up sending their children here." Eric told me that in the first year hosting the evening showcase they did not have the turnout they wanted because many parents simply don't have money for bus fare. Next year they are going to send school busses out to surrounding neighborhoods to bring parents to their open house events.

Although forward-leaning educators recognize the need for schools to change, and students value this kind of learning, it is often the parents who are the most afraid of making a nontraditional choice for their own children. Anya Smith-Roman and Emmy Schaeffer, two high school students in Atlanta who created their own Advanced Placement course, and about whom you will read more further on, think that parents will make better choices for their kids when they are more invested with what is going on at school on a daily basis. "For most parents," say Anya and Emmy, "their only real link to education is how they learned back when they were in school. What if we were collaborating with the parents from our own schools more? What if we used those connections for expanded internships? What if our parents took more of a role in exposing students to learning beyond the edge of campus? Sure, the students would benefit, but the parents would also get a frequent, firsthand view of what this kind of learning looks like and they would see that it leads to the sort of skills that are important in their own careers and lives. That is what most parents want for their students; they just don't know what it can look like."

Like any well-functioning marketplace, as school boundaries within and between districts are increasingly permeable, schools that offer a more engaged, exciting learning experience attract more demand than those that don't. For many schools, the simple act of storytelling plays a major role in developing the demand in the community for deeper learning experiences. Student-led workshops and exhibitions are often the best vehicle for conveying the difference between a traditional and a deeper learning classroom. I wandered around at a student-focused "STEM Exhibition Saturday" at Val Verde District south of Riverside, California, and saw the raw pride and wonder on the faces of parents and grandparents, almost none of whom had gone to college in this largely Latino and African American, working-class community. It was no surprise when I heard that, six months later, a district-wide evening college admissions workshop event had, in one year, gone from a few attendees to overflow and standing room only.

Regan Drew at Riverpoint Academy says that these events provide breakthrough moments for parents and others. "The visitors get it within minutes. They can't believe how much ownership the students have in their own learning. People get really emotional about it. In our community parents expect their kids to go on to college, and this was a big concern when we opened with a program that tested old traditions. Now we can show them that college acceptance is not going to be a problem. Demand is increasing every year," says Regan. "When we started we were accepting students from outside the district and now we have more applicants from inside the district than we have seats."

How We Will Press This Lever

Unlike government, big companies, or celebrities with millions of followers, most of us don't have the reach or power to create demand all at once. That is not how the successful schools and school leaders I found all over the country are enacting real change. They start by creating a forum for discussion and some shared ideas, and then they start to implement change, often one school at a time.

Starting Small

The wonderful thing about creating demand is that we all can press on this lever: in the classroom, conference room, faculty meeting, board meeting, Rotary Club, corporate retreat . . . anywhere with any size group of people who care about education. It doesn't matter if your school is highly traditional or starting to transform, if your community is wealthy or underserved, if your students are mostly college-bound or struggling to graduate. Creating demand is open to all because it starts with something we can all do: listen to each other.

Community Discussion

- Over a few months next school year, wherever members of your school community gather, hand out sticky notes or small blank cards and ask probing questions about the nature of great learning: What one word or words describe the conditions that lead to great learning? What does great teaching look like? What knowledge, skills, and outcomes do we want for our students to help them lead happy and productive lives after school? What excites your student about school? What is a drag? Take just three minutes and then gather up the notes. Sort the notes into similar "buckets," such as "pedagogy," "physical spaces," "student assessment," "people and their practices," or "essential skills." Each school will have a different set of buckets, and these help define great places to start work on pilots.

- Share the results with everyone in your school community. Have a community-wide discussion of the results. Is there a difference between what we *say we want* and what we *do*? Is there a difference between the experience we want for our students and their *actual* experience most days? If so, are we willing to change, or are we going to make excuses and point fingers? What can we change that aligns with our values and over which we have control?

- Distill what you have heard into a shared vision statement, what I call a "North Star of Great Learning," which outlines the major areas of agreement in the data you collect. Validate this through your community of educators, and courageously start pilots that, despite obstacles of novelty and uncertainty, most closely align what your school does with what great learning can be.

Community Inspiration

- Show *Most Likely to Succeed* or a similar movie followed by a community discussion about the movie. Advertise the event well in advance to your own families and the rest of the community. Get your parent's association involved in advertising and sponsoring the event. Include students in the event, because parents will always come to something if their own child is on the stage. Student leaders can give an introduction to the movie, help develop a list of essential questions for the discussion, or participate in a panel that leads the discussion. Make the events easy to attend, at times when working parents can gather, and perhaps even provide a bus for transportation if your families live in other neighborhoods.

- Build an element of community presentation or exhibition into new pilot programs as part of the student assessment process. Use your family networks to make these events, several times a year, something special that parents, grandparents, and friends attend, such as a major athletic contest or awards dinner. Send out a press release on one or two high-profile student projects to the local newspapers and TV stations.

Taking It to the Next Level

Once people in your community are talking about change, once there is even the start of a shared understanding that this kind of education is, in fact, better for our children than the old model, it is time to put some new ideas into practice. It is time, as I said in the introduction, to roll.

Pilot a New Program

- Create a highly visible program or partnership that engages students and boldly represents what is in your school's North Star of Great Learning. For example, you might build time into the schedule for passion-driven courses or convert a room into a low-tech maker space or studio for students to learn the power of original design and creativity.
- Gather a group of like-minded colleagues in a grade level or across the entire school, or among several schools, or between parents and business leaders and educators and students, pick a place to start, and *make a change*. Encourage the mind-set that sometimes it is OK to shift from "ready, aim, shoot" to the designers' credo: "ready, shoot, aim."
- Bring teachers from other classrooms, grade levels, or schools to see what "it" looks like in action. Start a "teachers teaching teachers" program for your scheduled professional development days so you build internal capacity as a learning organization based on peers, not outsiders. All teachers and their students who are running a pilot can put on a short workshop that enables others to see, question, and learn about some aspect of the program.

Show Off

- Share what you are doing as loudly as you can. Invite parents and community leaders into the school, shoot a video and post it on social media, and share it with educational thought leaders on social media or on well-known educational collaboration websites such as Edutopia.
- Don't waste your back-to-school night next year handing out syllabi on each class. Create an interactive showcase with parents, teachers, and students to demonstrate your vision for better learning and the excitement it creates among the students at your school.
- Always, always, show off your kids! Put passionate, engaged students at the center of who you are, what you do, and how you show it to others in your community. Nothing builds demand for a better path of learning than children who want to be there and are excited about their own learning. This is what creates demand: others seeing the possible, right there, in their neighborhood or city in a school that looks somewhat like their own. This is how people overcome their fears, which is largely what has kept them from doing what they wanted to do all along.

Finally, repeat, repeat, repeat. There is a powerful reason that you see the same advertisements time and time again on TV or billboards; they work. Be dogged and determined. If you are confident in the direction your school wants to take, you will win over many more advocates and supportive customers than just the early adopters. Develop a powerful student-centric message of the "why, what, and how of school change" grounded in what you heard from your own community of stakeholders, and stick to it!

CHAPTER THREE

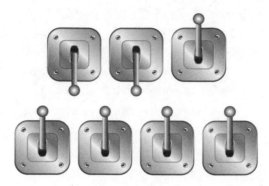

Lever #2
Build School-Community Learning Laboratories

Schools themselves have intellectual capital, but a city's ecosystem has so much more of it. Why are we keeping them so separate?

Michelle Cahill, Carnegie Corporation

If school is meant to prepare our students for the world, why do school and the world look and act so differently?

Bo Adams

A wandering visitor might have reasonably mistaken the Innovation Lab at Vista Innovation and Design Academy (VIDA) Middle School for an unused classroom-turned-storage space, one of those backwaters on campus where junk collects over the years until someone finally sneaks in on the weekend and tosses it all in a dumpster. Cabinets overflowed with old pieces of PVC, tin cans, torn cardboard boxes, half-used rolls of duct tape, cardboard toilet paper rolls, stacks of colored construction paper, and odd assortments of nails and screws. Three old, bulky computers sat on one corner table. Principal Eric Chagala smiled wanly when he showed off the lab's one small set of hand tools, the kind you might buy at Sears for $19.95.

VIDA, a public magnet school in Vista in the dry coastal hills about 40 minutes north of San Diego, converted from a poorly performing neighborhood school in 2014 to one of the most in-demand schools in the district in 2017. Within the district boundaries there are shaded, winding roads with widely spaced hacienda-style mansions and crowded commercial streets with big box shopping centers. But much of Vista reflects the largely Latino working class face of 21st century California: small stucco homes with brown yards on potholed streets that stand testament to the woeful stretching of public budgets. Virtually every student at VIDA qualifies for a free or reduced lunch, many are not native English speakers, and as many as 30% may be essentially homeless or in some kind of temporary or transitional living arrangement. The year before Eric and his team adopted an entirely new philosophy about teaching, learning, and their relationship to the community, test scores were low, truancy was high, parents rarely came to community meetings, and, as Eric says, "the police were here on average once per day" to deal with discipline issues. One year later, says Eric, "the cops have been on campus just once all year."

"When we opened the lab last year we brought students in, sat them down, and a teacher told them 'OK, your task is to build a trebuchet capable of launching a water balloon at a teacher.' The kids just sat there. A few minutes later she repeated the instruction and the kids still sat there, waiting for the instruction sheet. Finally, one girl raised her hand and asked, 'What is a trebuchet?' and we were off on a new kind of learning. Here we are just six months later and the students are imagining, creating, and building their own design challenges from scratch."

Then Eric told me the short story that still chokes me up when I retell it to audiences. "A few months after we opened the lab, I got a call to come to the front office. There was a mom wheeling a baby stroller full of this stuff that anyone would call trash—you know, tin cans, some PVC parts, some plastic bags. She didn't speak English so we got one of the staff [members] to come down and ask her what she wanted. She was crying and said she wanted to donate these supplies to the school because this was the first time in her life that she was ever able to contribute something to her child's education."

For most of the last 150 years, K–12 education has operated inside a compound with high, thick walls. The boundary between "school" and "world" has been more than just the edge of the sidewalk, the campus gate, or the door into the school building. The boundary has been physical, intellectual, social, and experiential. The pervasive message we have pounded into generations of students is that "you come to school to learn; after school you leave." The message we have pounded into teachers is "you have x minutes per day and week to fill your students with knowledge; close your door and keep them quiet and busy." The message we have pounded into parents is "the professional educators know what's best."

We know that students and teachers have lives outside of school, in a world where they spend two-thirds of their young lives, but intentionally and unintentionally we have kept our schools separate from that world. Sure, we go on field trips or bring in speakers on career day to share their stories and expertise for an hour or a day. We create short, safe, chaperoned service projects for students to periodically help in the community. But the deep, rich, colorful, messy palette of the world has not had a *real* place in our construct of "school." Needless to say, there are students for whom life outside of school is cruel and difficult; for them, school may be the single refuge in their lives, and we must value and preserve that. This chapter is not about damaging that necessary refuge; it is about learning *with* the world around us, not in spite of it.

Ronald Reagan's most famous quote was "Mr. Gorbachev, break down this wall!" referring to a physical barrier that separated democracy from dictatorship. Our students and teachers live behind a wall that separates them from the richest fields and veins of learning they will ever encounter: the world around them. Finally, those walls are beginning to crack. Educators, parents, students, and community stakeholders, including businesses that rely on our schools to prepare students as future employees and customers, increasingly recognize that breaching this artificial boundary is a profound win-win for all. For some schools and communities this means dusting off the centuries-old ideas of workplace apprenticeships. For others it is a set of multilateral partnerships among schools, colleges, and local business leaders that improves the funnel of students ready to succeed in college and the workforce. For still others it is a way for students to find relevance in the often dreary hours that they spend in school, tying what they learn to how they live . . . and how they can affect the lives of others beyond themselves.

This chapter could easily have been an entire book. Everywhere I looked I quickly and easily uncovered examples of public, private, and charter schools and districts, nonschool partners, and even entire cities breaching the boundary between school and world; it is an inexorably rising tide. The only limiting factors seem to be imagination and fear of the lesser known. As I interviewed educators who are building these partnerships, I found enormously high levels of passion, enthusiasm, and, most important, optimism that we have rediscovered a critical key to engaging students in the relevance of their own learning. I also found the perfect on-ramp for non-educators who care deeply about our kids and their future to jump in as part of a dynamic, fun, rewarding solution to the problem of stagnant education.

Although there is no one template of success among the schools and networks you will see in this chapter, there is one powerful through-going theme: *we have rediscovered the fuel of intrinsic motivation.* If there is a single fatal symptom in the flawed system of traditional education it is the lack of relevance that students feel for the reason behind what they are doing for all of those hours, days, and years at school; what it means to them to do well on a test or why they should work so hard to get a few better grades than they got last year; and what that struggle means for their future. Lacking clarity of this relevance, students lack engagement, the key link in effective learning that we have known about since at least the era of John Dewey. Through the many ways that schools are building powerful bonds between "school" and "not school," they are engaging students in an understanding of relevance for their own education.

> *If there is a single fatal symptom in the flawed system of traditional education it is the lack of relevance that students feel for the reason behind what they are doing for all of those hours, days, and years at school . . .*

The smearing of boundaries between school and community is already here, at least for some communities and some families. As school budgets have been hit hard in the last decade, other learning options have quickly arisen to fill the gap, providing extracurricular programs outside of the traditional school. Jal Mehta from the Harvard Graduate School of Education says that "parents and students tell us that all of the interesting stuff happens outside of school, at the community center on weekends and during the summer. Parents are paying for regular school through their taxes and then paying again for these supplementary experiences, if they can afford it. At this point, there is nothing equitable about it, but there is nothing stopping this market from evolving." Mehta says that this trend has already taken firm hold in areas with wealthier families. "It is just happening," says Mehta. "There does not have to be formal coordination. There is a large market that is just going to evolve on its own. Hopefully we will see public funding follow this lead in order to broaden access."

Chris Jackson of Big Picture Learning, a network of schools that has pioneered student internships with community partners, says that authentic learning outside of schools is rooted in deep, ongoing, sustainable, multilateral relationships. Big Picture Learning schools, many of which look demographically a lot like VIDA in Vista Unified or like Design Lab Early High School in Cleveland, have inserted their students into the business community as a core part of their learning ethos for more than 20 years. "Seventy percent of Big Picture Learning school students who *don't* go on to college end up getting a job through their internship project," Chris says, "because these are deep, multiyear commitments; they are really about building relationships and community, and those are huge advantages when it comes to getting a first job out of school."

Designing for the Real World

Sometimes great ideas start really small and are just too good to *not* grow. Don Buckley is a veteran teacher in New York City and was one of the early pioneers of design thinking in education. He partnered in a new venture to bring design thinking–style learning programs to K–12 schools with Rinat Aruh, who had formerly worked on educational products with the large office supplies chain Staples. They suggested to Staples that, in the best tradition of user-centric design, the company might want to get some actual students involved in thinking about new products for the home and school. One of the lead designers at Staples loved the idea and funded Don and Rinat's "Tools at Schools" program to work with two schools in underserved communities, MS88 in Brooklyn and Ron Clark Academy in Atlanta.

Don and Rinat had worked with schools on design projects in the past, but "the merchant piece had been missing," Don told me. "Staples saw an opportunity to take these student prototypes all the way to production levels and take them to market." The first set of products hit the shelves at Staples stores in 2015 and another round came out in 2016 with more planned, including a newly designed portable student work desk and a new style of binders. Staples sees so much potential in getting student users involved in their product design that they have already added three more schools in Manhattan and Austin, Texas. "The product is the hook to catch people's interest," Don says. "It is pretty amazing and really cool for students and their families to walk into a store and be able to say 'We made that!'"

As a designer, Don knows that there is no one recipe that is going to work at every school. "We might pitch the idea of taking a product to market to an entire school of students, but it is up to the school if we engage with one grade level, or one small group, and if the work is done during the school day or after hours. What is really important is that this kind of authentic, real-world project gets the teachers to ask for professional development on how they can build the learning style into their regular courses. Over time this will be an experience that really helps to change school culture. A real key is to find those one or two people on each side— the merchant and the school—who are willing to take a risk and support this kind of partnership."

Spreading Student Confidence in the Thinkabit Lab

Like Don and Rinat, Ed Hidalgo had an idea, saw an opportunity, and just ran with it as far as those above him at the telecommunications giant Qualcomm would allow. Ed worked in hiring and workforce development at Qualcomm for 17 years and had developed programs to help employees find their own professional strengths and weaknesses. Several years ago Ed asked, "What if we could apply what we know about helping *employees* find their passion to helping *students* get motivated at a much younger age?" A small team designed and built what is now the Thinkabit Lab, a clean, open, incubator-like conference-laboratory-classroom suite in the heart of the Qualcomm campus, where middle school students can come for a day and, says Don, "think about their future, possible careers, and what is coming in their lives. We want them to design, think, program, and build circuits, and then turn all of that into a unique product . . . in just a few hours." According to Don, many of the students who visit the lab have never thought about what lies past school and they certainly have never been taught how to approach this problem in their schools. "Every student is starting at the pole position. We want them all to see that they belong; that they have a place and real value in the world. And we want them to just tinker and play and create something really cool and sort of crazy so they leave thinking of learning as a lot of fun."

The demand for the Thinkabit Lab from local schools has been overwhelming. In just the first 18 months that the lab was open, more than 6,000 middle school students and 3,000 other visitors experienced this unique combination of life preparation, coding, building, and all-hands fun. The day I visited the lab, I met Jackie Luzak, a principal with the local Cajon Valley Union District. Her students were cutting, gluing, and wiring wildly spinning robots made out of pieces of old dolls, Legos, glitter, and plastic toys. They had programmed the little bots to spin and bob and wave arms, even though few of the students had ever programmed in the past. The lab was a circus of color, energy, and noise, and every student was going to leave at the end of that single day having helped design and build a fully functioning computer-driven machine. Jackie has had several groups visit the lab, including with her superintendent and board of trustees. After seeing the level of student engagement and experiencing the lab themselves, Jackie says that teachers have dug into in the pedagogy behind the program, and new thinking has begun to percolate through the district. Jackie has been able to build interdisciplinary teacher teams that now lead students through combined math, English, and engineering projects. Every student at her school now spends an hour a day for 12 weeks working on projects they design and build. According to Jackie the pedagogy that is on display at the lab has become mainstream at her school, not just something that happens in a maker space one period a day.

Impacts from the Thinkabit Lab have branched way out from just the lab space on Qualcomm's corporate campus. Ed secured funding from the parent company for massive high-tech upgrades to innovation maker spaces in local schools, including VIDA's Innovation Lab. In just their third year, the kids and teachers at VIDA have cleared the shelves of tin cans and toilet paper rolls, the three old computers, and one set of hand tools to make space for Arduino boards, Lego blocks, soldering sets, and Chromebooks.

Partnering with a Giant

Although the Qualcomm experiment has had an impact on learners at many schools, another large corporate partner is trying to affect one school in a profound way. D-Tech High School is a relatively new public charter school within the San Mateo Union High district, just west of the runways at the San Francisco Airport. Their charter includes a flexible daily schedule that allows students to explore a wide array of individual interests, so school leaders put out a call to the community for volunteers with special "super powers" to come in and team-teach alongside certificated faculty members. Several employees at the main campus of nearby high-tech giant Oracle volunteered to co-teach electives in programming and computer science. According to D-Tech's founding executive director, Ken Montgomery, the experience convinced some senior people at Oracle that "if you really want to invest in education for the future you have to go deep. They got excited about this kind of education and asked what we needed. We needed a building of our own, and in this area land is extremely expensive. So they are building a school building for us on their own corporate campus land."

Oracle found that, although the investment in the building is critical, even more so is the investment they are making with their people. As the new D-Tech campus grows, employees will be intimately involved with the school. "The volunteer teachers from Oracle get released from their regular work for the time they need to be with us and Oracle is paying for that time," says Ken. "It is an incredible resource. A professional working in a field can explain things to a student in ways a teacher might not be able to." And not all community volunteers at D-Tech High are techies from Oracle. As the school has proven the success of the volunteer co-teacher model, other community groups have partnered with teachers to offer an enriched curriculum that other budget-strapped public schools can replicate. Bank officers from Wells Fargo are leading a financial literacy course. Actors from a local theater company help teach drama. Dance and yoga teachers whose private practice is mostly during after-school hours have free time during the day so they can come work at the school, some as volunteers and others for a stipend. Ken says that this community outsourcing is a highly efficient way to combine resources, but "it takes humility and flexibility on both sides. We have to be very flexible with our use of time so we can take advantage of outsiders when they are available. And our community partners know they are not going to come in and run the school; we have full autonomy to ensure that we are meeting our mission for the students."

Going to Scale

What if you don't know a creative innovator such as Don Buckley, and what if your city or town doesn't have a high-tech giant to partner with? Although the creative and collaborative inspiration of single people, schools, or companies make for great prototypes, what is potentially game shattering are the larger schools, districts, networks, and communities that have been breaching the boundaries between school and world at scale, some of them for more than a decade. The few I write about here are just the very tip of a marvelously growing iceberg of win-win partnerships in which we all can play impactful roles.

> *Although the creative and collaborative inspiration of single people, schools, or companies make for great prototypes, what is potentially game shattering are the larger schools, districts, networks, and communities that have been breaching the boundaries between school and world at scale . . .*

A Learning Revolution in Pittsburgh

I admit I was surprised to find a hotspot of ground-breaking school-community partnership innovation in Pittsburgh, a city at the heart of the American rustbelt and hard hit by unfriendly changes in the global and national economies since the 1990s. But it was exactly that challenge—the need to reinvent the region to attract industries and families with well-paying jobs—that led to the creation of the Remake Learning Network in the greater Pittsburgh area. The network started in 2007 with support from local and regional foundations as an effort to improve K–12 educational experiences and student performance through an expansion of active learning pedagogy. Almost a decade later it now encompasses more than 200 separate organizations and 2,000 individuals from schools, museums, universities, after-school programs, and libraries to entrepreneurial start-ups, high-tech labs, and high-rise, white collar companies that had never thought about the value of deep partnerships with inner-city high school kids.

According to the "Remake Learning Playbook," which is available for free download, "teachers and administrators work with designers and technologists to collaboratively develop new course curricula." The goal is to create opportunities on and off school campuses for students to "develop their own interests, to work collaboratively to find creative solutions to problems, and to experiment, fail, and start over with new ideas." Remake Learning based their model on the Innovation Education Clusters work of Harvard Business School's Michael Porter, who demonstrated that interconnected ecosystems of companies, suppliers, and educational institutions raise the productivity of individual organizations as well as that of the entire region.

Through the Remake Learning Network, students study, learn, and work in off-campus settings from museums to high-tech maker spaces, and their teachers bring new perspectives from those experiences back to the classroom. Higher education partners "provide critical evaluation resources" to help the K–12 educators track and test how these new approaches actually work, or not, in terms of student performance. Small companies and entrepreneurial incubators organize meet-ups and "design jams" where professionals, teachers, and students share ideas about how they might retool the learning experience to more closely reflect real-world challenges, while covering standards-based content.

For one of the local educators who helped design Remake Learning, there is enormous tangible proof at the school, classroom, and student level that the network produces real results. Lisa Palmieri is the head of Holy Family Academy, a novel independent Catholic high school that draws most of its students from the city's urban core. Every student at Holy family participates in a four-year Corporate Work Study Program, spending one full day per week working at a partner company or organization. The students are actually part-time employees of these companies, and the money they make pays the majority of their modest high school tuition. The students select an entry-level track: administration, research, accounting, HR, office services, finance, IT, marketing, and business development. Each student reports to a supervisor who makes quarterly assessments of the student's progress and performance, scored and narrative, on six life-critical competencies: listening, patience, organization, quality of work, time management, and communication.

Lisa says the program creates a powerful combination of experiential learning in academic-related projects with the skills that students need to succeed beyond high school . . . particularly students who have grown up in poverty. "A lot of our students are inner city kids and there is skepticism that they can go work on the 60th floor of a building downtown. But the fact is that they can. They get business work experience, marketable skills, a network of business contacts, a wide exposure to career opportunities, and a chance to build and refine work ethic and their self-esteem." Lisa says that one of the real benefits is that the students "are seeing people who look like them, particularly women and racial minorities, working in fields like STEM; frankly, it is hard for schools to hire diverse faculty [members] in some of these areas." The program also frees the regular school teachers up for one full day every week when the students are at their internships, valuable time they can use, Lisa says, to "grow as a learning community and get better at teaching the students within a paradigm that combines the classroom and the larger community."

Schools win in many ways when they can access this kind of resource at scale. Lisa's small school does not have significant public or private resources to draw on. "Our students go to the Carnegie Mellon Fab Lab every week," says Lisa, "so we don't have to invest tens or hundreds of thousands of dollars ourselves in building out that kind of lab. The students are in a college environment that we could never replicate on our own campus." Because this is a city- and region-wide collaborative, the range of experiences open to students is enormous, says Lisa. "This year we had students prototyping solutions to problems in their own communities that they identified, which is huge when it comes to keeping students engaged and understanding the relevance of their schoolwork. Or they might interact with the Manchester Craftsmen's Guild where they rotate through four art-design trade studios during the year. Or they can take 'Tools, Skills, and Measures' taught by actual tradespeople from the community." Lisa and Remake Learning are even putting together a badging and credentialing program in which students from many schools can get credit, some for college, and résumé-building certifications for a range of programs from across the entire region, so proof of their learning and expertise is not restricted to where they might be registered at school. They have even created a system of iTunes-like playlists of potential learning experiences that correlate with workforce needs in the region, so students and their families can customize a personal track of community-based learning options.

A Deep and Broad Community Commitment

Every day, 11th- and 12th-grade students from the Clovis and Fresno Unified School Districts in California's Central Valley jump on a bus and take the short cross-town trip to the Center for Advanced Research and Technology (CART), a 75,000-square-foot building that feels more like a high-tech business park than a high school. The students attend half-day classes in laboratories designed for career-specific tracks that breach traditional subject silos: science, engineering, communications, and global economics. The project-based courses incorporate a meld of advanced English, science, math, and technology and are taught by teams of instructors from education and local businesses. The CART course catalog sounds like an exciting college brochure: biomedicine, engineering and product development, law and order and policy, robotics and electronics, marketing and advertising, psychology and human behavior.

Now in its 16th year, CART supports about 15% of all high school students in the two adjacent school districts that serve distinctly different populations, according to CEO Rick Watson. Students take classes at their regular schools to augment the range of classes at CART. Rick says that CART represents "the future of college and career education. Sure, we feel that we are producing good citizens through a program that merges rigor, relevance, and personalized learning, but what is most important is that our students gain the confidence that they are prepared for college and the workplace." The structure of CART breaks boundaries that restrict students in more traditional schools. "The classes are very collaborative and team-project-based," says Rick. "We get students coming to CART with 1.0 GPAs and we get students who are taking five Advanced Placement classes. Fresno has one of the highest poverty rates in the state and Clovis has a much higher economic demographic. We put those students all on the same team. This is one opportunity for students from very different backgrounds to work and learn together. What we have created is much more like a college atmosphere than a traditional high school. Students have a lot of freedom during their time here that they don't get in their regular school, and they learn to use that freedom wisely." In addition to the business-professional interactions during the day, CART currently has seven courses that are tracked for credit at Fresno State University, and several more in which students garner credit at the local community colleges.

What is most exciting about a CART-like model is the depth and breadth of support across the community, not just among students and teachers; this is a field that is wide open for impactful participation by almost anyone. Rick told me that in 2016 about 300 mentors from local businesses will participate, from guest speaker to classroom mentor to taking students into the field and hosting internships. About 100 local companies and organizations are involved in some level of ongoing financial support. Although the operating funding, primarily for the teaching staff, comes from the two districts and the County Office of Education, many of the local companies that send people to work at CART provided initial capital to build out the labs and make annual grants to pay for tools, materials, and supplies. In a part of the California Central Valley that has been almost exclusively associated with the local farming industry for more than a century, CART provides a facility and an academic program where students reach beyond the bounds of a seven-subject assembly line to collaborate with professional partners from the local, national, and even international business communities.

One School, One Community, One at a Time

Atlanta has the dubious honor of being the most economically segregated major city in America. In 2013, Raj Chetty and others at Harvard published a map of America showing where our citizens and neighbor-hoods are most segregated by economics, which they found was the greatest inhibitor of upward mobility toward the vanishing American dream. Atlanta took the "top" spot, so it is particularly important that a wealthy suburban independent school is planting a satellite campus in the urban Atlanta core and creating an entirely new learning experience among teach-ers and students who, unfortunately, would never have come together in the usual course of their lives and learning. Opened in 2017, Lab Atlanta is a semester-long academic program for high school sophomores from the greater Atlanta area that will empower a mixture of students from very diverse backgrounds to dive deeply into problems that challenge Atlanta as a community. Founder Laura Deisley of the private Lovett School says that they decided to locate the school in collaboration with the Savannah College of Art and Design in Midtown Atlanta to allow a completely immersive proximity to the heart of the metro area. The program will mix design and innovation into a more traditional set of courses so students can stay on track to return to their regular schools, but they can also get a completely different experience from seeing, finding, and studying prob-lems and designing solutions relevant to the larger community.

Lab Atlanta will be a model of shared sustainability: a third of the students will be able to afford the full tuition of about $12,000; a third will be able to afford about half of that; and the remaining third will be provided full scholarships. This model of equity requires corporate fund-ing, and at this point, Laura says, her door is being "knocked down" by everyone from the mayor's office, to large companies such as ATT, to partners such as Emory University. "It takes a density of voices and opin-ions to get something like this that will really have traction," says Laura. "The best thing we can have is enough community connections to allow us to explore the edges of what it really means to learn in a community-immersed environment."

Finally, I reached out to someone who for decades has been deeply embedded in the interweave of schools, justice, equity, and community. Chris Thinnes has been a teacher, administrator, trainer, writer, and is cur-rently on the national board of the Progressive Education Network. He steered me to his always eloquent blog posts where he highlighted two schools that, in very different ways and very different worlds, have largely dissolved the traditional barriers between school and community.

In the heart of the Bronx, Chris says, Cornerstone Academy for Social Action (CASA) Middle School has built an entire curriculum on "student inquiry and activism about issues that affect their community." To build those skills that most schools claim are key to a 21st century education, CASA students develop projects on themes of drug use, domestic violence, and economic inequality that, unfortunately, are pervasive in their community and in their own lives. They steer curriculum toward, not around, current events that demand their attention, and use their voices to share with the world what they learn, observe, and know. The results of this deep immersion into immediate relevancy is extraordinary, Chris says, even when measured with traditional metrics—90% of CASA's students, who are racially diverse and largely underserved, come to CASA performing below grade level, and, in a program that is decidedly not focused on test preparation, "demonstrated the highest combined growth score average among all of New York City's more than 1,800 public schools" on 2014 state-mandated exams.

They steer curriculum toward, not around, current events that demand their attention, and use their voices to share with the world what they learn, observe, and know.

At the other end of the country, far away from innovation labs, STEM mash-ups, high-rises, urban blight, and big corporate campuses, Chris talks about a small school in the rural hills of Hawaii that we all might wish to visit someday, where teachers and staff members "take to the streets at the beginning of every school year to learn and relearn how they can best meet the needs of their families." The Nānākuli school serves more than 400 students in the federally protected Native Hawaiian Homesteads on the western shore of O'ahu. Chris reports that every year, five-member teams from the school meet with families and other community stakeholders to not only find out what they need but also what they, the families and community, can contribute back to the education of the children whom they all share and serve. Every morning of the school year, the students, teachers, and school leaders gather in an assembly to celebrate and reflect on their links to their history and ancestors and "when each morning a school leader calls out 'where does learning happen,' the students call out in unison 'learning happens everywhere!'"

How We Will Press This Lever

During the heart of the Progressive Era of American education, John Dewey founded the Laboratory School at the University of Chicago in order to connect a center of knowledge, the university, with a center of deeper learning, the Lab School. We have the opportunity to reimagine the "lab school" of the 21st century. The centers of knowledge today are *vastly* more distributed than they were 120 years ago. Knowledge, experience, and creativity are not hidden behind ivy-covered walls; they abound across a social-economic-community web that includes huge corporations, small businesses, public institutions, laboratories and research centers, individual entrepreneurs, not-for-profits, and the student-teacher team working on a design project at their school. The problems that are relevant to everyone across this web are profound and thus intrinsically excite us each to learn in order to help solve them. We just need to connect students and teachers much more closely with the rich, available learning that we find all around us, beyond the classroom walls.

Starting Small

- Create a simple maker space at your school, and commit that "making" will start with student-generated ideas and questions related to their own interests and lives outside of school. Starting a maker space with things such as cardboard, PVC, Legos, and other basic materials is simple (there are plenty of free how-to resources online); making that connection between students and their lives and interests is a critical element that many schools fail to include.
- Look for learning opportunities right outside the classroom, on and off campus. Learning on a short walk can start with observation and reflection, which leads to asking questions and collaboratively framing problems and finding solutions. Students and teachers might start with a walk around the campus or the neighborhood near school, a brainstorm of what is most important to students, or a visit to local gardens, parks, farms, businesses, or downtown areas. Search on keywords "expeditionary learning" for ideas on how to get started.
- Find one community partner willing to work with teachers and students on and off campus to create new learning opportunities that

connect content with problems that students find relevant to their lives. Reach out to your parent body and local business and service organizations for that first willing partner to start a pilot program. Start with one teacher and one class or grade level. Find another school in your city or region that already has a community learning program and learn what worked for them.

Taking It to the Next Level

Many students learn in their communities through infrequent field trips and brief community service projects. Many schools have one or two teachers who have started small, and that is as far as the school ever gets. If we want to really change learning, we have to scale up these great starting points, which really just means expanding on what is already working for so many schools around the country.

Expand Partnerships

- Once you have a pilot partnership to show, reach out to a larger, more diverse set of community organizations (museums, libraries, service organizations, nonprofits, colleges, large and small locally owned businesses). Ask for their time, and their people's time, not just financial donations. Research how other schools have structured effective internships and teaching partnerships and come to the table with some ideas about what would be most exciting for your students and teachers.
- Join or form a citywide or regional consortium of schools and community partners along the lines of Remake Learning or CART. Use this larger group to secure funding that includes professional development for your teachers on how to incorporate off-campus learning into the standard curriculum.
- Tackle the issue of time at your school. Students and teachers will need time during the day that might not fit into 50-minute blocks. Think about team-teaching relationships that might allow one teacher to monitor a large class of students working on their projects while the other takes students for a learning walk or to the maker space.

Focus on Big All-School Themes

- Adopt student-generated big themes on which learning will take place at your entire school for a year or even longer. Similar to student elections, allow students to research, discuss, nominate, and vote for themes that are important to them and relevant to their lives outside of school.
- Offer stipends for teachers to develop or find open source curriculum around the all-school themes; this is a great ask for funding from your community partners. Don't require that these new curricula need to be fully baked in the first year; let that first year be an evolutionary pilot with students helping to test what does and does not work, and refine for future years.

Do these challenges appear daunting? Who will take the lead? How will we organize? How do we get started? Where does the funding come from, and who makes decisions? Fortunately, there are many up-and-running examples from pioneers who have already broken the ground, and they are more than willing to share their experiences. I have found that by constantly asking two questions, you will find more opportunities to break the boundaries between school and the world than you can imagine:

- How might we cover content in a more engaging way if we left the classroom?
- How might students be more involved in creating the themes and projects within which they will learn critical content?

Schools are not someone else's problem. Schools are part of *our* community no matter what hat you wear. Unfortunately, our system gives power to those who try to affect learning by harassing the principal or taking over the school board when there are so many more powerful ways to positively affect our students' futures. Anyone who is frustrated by the forces that have skewed education in a way you think is counterproductive can press this lever with time, energy, brainpower, and treasure. As educators, we need to find these willing and eager partners and include them in the work they want to do!

CHAPTER FOUR

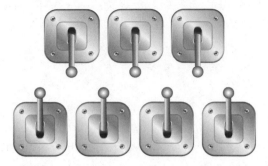

Lever #3
Encourage Open Access to Knowledge

Next time you open the paper, and you see an intellectual property decision, a telecom's decision, it's not about something small and technical. It is about the future of the freedom to be as social beings with each other, and the way information, knowledge and culture will be produced.

Yochai Benkler, Harvard Law School

There is a limit on how much information you can keep bottled up.

Dick Gregory

The WiFi slowed and then died, never a good sign at an educational technology conference, but keynoter Alan November never missed a beat. This was the day I first heard about Wolfram Alpha, a window into a world where answers to questions are just another commodity, like a can of soup on the shelf to be grabbed and tossed into my cart, not the magic key to grade promotion, admission to college, or a better starting salary at your first job. For those many readers who have never heard of Wolfram Alpha, it is a free site that can answer pretty much any question or solve any computable problem that you or your children or employees or students might imagine. Not only that; it can show you, step-by-step, how it reached the answer. When a future Mr. Spock is standing on the *bridge of the starship* Enterprise *chatting with a soothing, all-knowing computer, the roots of that conversation will be in the kind of thinking that designed Wolfram Alpha.*

At one point, Alan asked how many of the educators in the room knew about Wolfram Alpha and knew that it was being used in their schools. About half raised their hands. I am not a techie, so I forgave my own ignorance, but I was shocked that so many in the room were similarly hearing about such a seemingly Oz-like powerful knowledge source for the very first time. One teacher then told us that his school blocked access to Wolfram Alpha with its campus firewall. A vocal minority of the teachers at his school had rebelled at allowing students to access a site that could do their problem sets for them. A dozen others in the room said that their schools had similar policies. There was a gasp around the room, some shaking heads in bewilderment. How do we decide to block access to knowledge on a school campus when that same knowledge is available to our students as soon as they set foot on the sidewalk? How do we insist that the way we have done things in the past—worksheets, problem sets, homework assignments—is still valid, when the entire world is undergoing a fundamental change in the relationship between people and the controls of knowledge? How do schools, whose fundamental mission is learning, cringe in the face of inevitable evolution in the nature and process of that learning? How, ultimately, can we not embrace and find ways to leverage more access to knowledge, not less?

In an industrial-age system of education known for rigidity, there is nothing that screams "one-size-fits-all" more than the box of clean, new, unscuffed, tightly bound, inky-smelling textbooks that arrives in a teacher's room once every five or six years, accompanied by an instruction manual about how to efficiently transfer the information in those boxes to groups of students. Similar to holy tomes copied by Middle Age monks, these textbooks are one-way transfer points, mostly purchased with your precious tax dollars from a small oligarchy of publishers to whom we have collectively ceded control over what our students need to know. Because these books will be used for several years, students are not allowed to underline or highlight the text or jot notes in the margins, skills we *know* help learners to actually learn. The material in the book might be out-of-date; some of the books were written years ago and "updated" as the publishers see fit. The material in the book used by students in Maine might have been massaged or factually compromised by politically motivated state review committees in places such as Texas or California, because those huge, monolithic markets can drive what is actually delivered by the publishers to every district in every other state. Billions of dollars are spent out of the public coffers each year. Deeper learning principles are ignored or violated. Young students bend under the bulky weight of stuffed backpacks, like Sherpas on a Himalayan trail, hauling thick volumes home only to "read pages 100–106 for the quiz tomorrow" or "do the odd-numbered problems at the end of the chapter."

The entire process is positively medieval . . . and it is an unnecessary, wasteful, easily avoided obstruction to deeper learning for students and teachers. Simply, textbooks are the instruction manuals of outmoded education. They tell the teacher, "Do the exact same thing you did last year, and the year before . . . until we change the book for you." They tell the students, "Just learn what is in here, at the rate at which your teacher tells you to turn the page or read the chapter, know this stuff when the exam is put in front of you, and you will be OK." They enforce a false narrative that success in the world is about mastering the art of knowing what is in a book, just like the instruction binder that used to be required reading for an entry-level worker on an assembly line in the age before even assembly line jobs required thought, judgment, and collaboration. Are there times when those binders are important, when standard books and manuals hold really important information that students, teachers, and workers need to know? Of course! But there are times when none of that is true, and many schools are still stuck in the "it's all in the book" mode.

. . . textbooks are the instruction manuals of outmoded education.

In this chapter we will look at the rapid democratization of learning tools through the use of open educational resources (OER), and the obstacles that still block and seek to artificially control that access. Pressing this lever, of widening access for our learners to broader, not narrower, sources of knowledge, of pursuing dynamic exploration over perennial stasis, should be the easiest challenge in this book, and one in which *we all* can participate with almost magical ease. It is, after all, a next logical progression in the sharing of information, from the printing press that took knowledge out of the hands of the Church, to the Internet that brought personal access to information into billions of hands, to people such as Sal Khan and the audacious assumption that the value of teaching lies not in the knowledge itself but in the open and free provision of that knowledge and how to use it.

The Rise of Open Educational Resources

Teachers have been able to create their own content for decades. Some of us are old enough to remember the worksheets cranked out on clanking, smelly mimeograph machines; more of us grew up in the era of stapled packets from the Xerox copier, much of which was probably illegally pirated against overlooked copyright laws. The OER movement of today is an enormous advance from those piecemeal copy-and-staple days. Broadly speaking, OER are digital learning and teaching resources that have been prepared, reviewed, vetted, and compiled, and are *freely available* under open licenses. Let me repeat that for readers who are not directly involved in our schools; these resources are *free*. OER include everything from videos, articles, project outlines, and study guides to fully scaffolded curriculum just as it would be found in a textbook. Many of the major OER have been developed by accredited teachers to fully meet state standards. They are free for teachers and students—anyone in fact—to use, shuffle, embellish, edit, revise, and share.

Andrew Marcinek, who in 2016 was the open education advisor of the US Department of Education, says that the growth and availability of OER are not meant to suggest that teachers must now all create entire new textbooks on their own. "It is about taking what you have and organizing it in a way that gives students a variety of access points to your content" (Edutopia, 2013). The resources are vastly more flexible than a standard textbook, Andrew says. "What we are doing is giving our faculty and our students more ways to connect and share dynamic, developing content. Teachers can change and update content when they need to," rather than relying on, and waiting for, an archaic publication stream, controlled by a few state review committees and potentially years out-of-date at any point in time.

OER have been around for about 15 years, and although adoption has been slow and spotty, we may well be close to a tipping point. Mega companies are pushing into the OER market with 2016 launches such as the clearinghouse for educational resources of Amazon Inspire and free-access virtual reality content via Google Expeditions. A white paper published by the Council of Chief State School Officers in 2014 found that 26 states were using or promoting OER, 20 states were planning OER initiatives,

15 states were considering options for districts and schools to develop their own OER, and 7 states were considering OER as a replacement for traditional instructional materials. Tom Van der Ark, interviewed by Julie Wilson for the Woodrow Wilson Foundation study on future trends in K–12 education, says that teachers informally building OER for use with classroom learning management systems has "led to a bottom-up revolution" in how we structure access to knowledge for our students. "The fact that you can create a free resource . . . is quite remarkable. Most superintendents and school boards and state chiefs and policy makers still do not appreciate how important that bottom-up phenomenon of digital, free, open resources is."

Although just a few years ago OER were largely the purview of a few free-range teachers and progressive schools, they have rapidly become mainstream in some districts and states. Rebecca Kockler, assistant superintendent of academic content at the Louisiana Department of Education, says that in transitioning to Common Core Standards and curriculum "we went through a real shift in our expectations for students. We decided that at the state level we needed to be involved in supporting change at the level of actual teaching and learning, not just broad policy." She says that they wrapped their approach to change around three major points of leverage: curriculum, assessment, and professional development. "First we had to get curriculum right," says Rebecca. "We are a 'choice' state; districts are allowed to purchase whatever materials they want, but we wanted to create easy pathways for districts to approve the highest quality materials. We looked at hundreds of programs and ranked them by quality and the best alignment to the standards. We signed a statewide contract with the top-tier vendors so the districts could say 'I don't have to go through a five-month contracting process' in order to get the best materials into the hands of the users."

Two of those top-tier sources that Louisiana reviewed were Eureka Math and EngageNY, both of which are OER. Rebecca says that "in two years we have gone from 20% of our districts using top-tier OER to 80%." Although some districts use OER because they save money, Rebecca says that was not their first consideration, particularly in a state where not all of their schools can take advantage of a fully digital resource. "Where there is a huge difference," says Rebecca, "is in the marketplace of vendors who can supply professional development in support of OER. If you buy a book from a publisher, you essentially have one source of professional training for your teachers. If you use OER, there are many more tools in the marketplace, including some new virtual vendors that are particularly helpful to our more remote, rural districts." As districts became more comfortable with OER, they "realized we needed to create our own tools since the publishing industry wasn't changing fast enough. So we built our own comprehensive literacy curriculum for K–12 teachers. Our districts are seeing faster growth in student performance, principal support grounded in strong collaboration, and teacher support focused on content. When districts integrate these layers, performance growth happens faster."

There has been an explosion of for-profit and not-for profit sources for OER in the last few years as first thousands, and now millions, of teachers are gaining comfort in a world where their curriculum does not come bound in a standard textbook. One of the leaders in the OER revolution is the K–12 OER Collaborative. CEO Larry Singer says that OER empower a critical transformation from just "doing" education to actually knowing "what and why." At least since the late 1980s, says Larry, teachers have largely been trained in content delivery and classroom management, not in the skills of how to develop effective pedagogy and instructional design. "Publishers package teaching guidelines and instructional models in their textbooks," says Larry. "The instructional model is basically in the table of contents of their books. Teachers get a box of books at the start of the year, and the teacher's edition, and they just follow along." The use of OER empowers and demands teachers to actually consider *what* they are doing and *why they are doing it*, which is an enormous step in building the type of growth mind-set that is so critical to a deeper learning model

The use of OER both empowers and demands teachers to actually consider what *they are doing and* why they are doing it, *which is an enormous step in building the type of growth mind-set that is so critical to a deeper learning model.*

One of the most popular sources for OER, EngageNY offers an enormous library of curriculum and other resources, spanning all grade levels and subjects of K–12. They are building a huge user base way beyond the original target market in New York state. According to staff at

UnboundED, which spun off from EngageNY to offer OER on a national basis, they have had more than 200 million page views as of early 2016. And, according to a national Rand Corporation study (Opfer et al., 2016), 44% of math teachers who responded were accessing EngageNY free math resources on at least a weekly basis. Larry Singer credits early developers such as EngageNY who "pushed us into a new environment. Teachers suddenly needed to be involved in developing the pedagogy and instructional practice, the interactions, the full program." The approach found fertile ground among teachers and administrators who were looking for ways to align with a deeper, more individualized learning experience for our students. "K–12 OER [are] stepping on the shoulders of these early pioneers," says Larry. "We are developing content, materials, and services that are high quality, meet new and differentiated learning needs, and are engaging [with] both students and teachers. We don't want teachers to just open the box and use it; we want them to engage, customize, localize, and augment from a basic foundation or framework that we can start them with. Our approach is completely the opposite of that of the major publishers and traditional textbooks."

The Problems of OER

If OER offer such clear benefits, why do so many districts still rely on standard published textbooks and materials? It seems that schools and districts, struggling under crushing budget restrictions, would just be *leaping* at the chance to save money and upgrade their product at the same time. TJ Bliss at the Hewlett Foundation says that the use of materials such as textbooks is usually not a teacher decision in public schools. "Districts decide about the adoption of materials and texts, and many are resistant to use OER as [they do] not fit into their traditional approval and purchasing practices," TJ says. "The cost savings are often not an incentive for districts, because if they save money on materials, texts, and curriculum, in some cases they have to give that money back to the state and cannot repurpose it for something else." Let me repeat; according to the Hewlett Foundation, one

Many districts don't take advantage of free, valuable, fully accredited materials purely because of arcane purchasing practices.

of the leading nonprofit education organizations in the country, many districts don't take advantage of free, valuable, fully accredited materials purely because of arcane purchasing practices.

Larry Singer agrees that schools are by nature conservative institutions. "The question is how to manage change in systems like this. Education does not have the plasticity of other markets like health care or technology. Decisions are institutionalized in a highly controlled, government-regulated system," says Larry, but he sees some of those obstacles starting to crumble. "Over the last seven to eight years, most states have changed their definitions that govern how they can spend money on instructional resources. It used to be that money for 'instructional supplies' was pretty restricted to text- and workbooks. Now those budgets can be spent on a huge range of materials, supplies, support, equipment, and instructional services. Districts now have the option to look at which sources provide the best return on investment to the learning experience."

Kate Gerson of UnboundED cites two big obstacles to OER adoption. The first is that "adults don't know what we need to know about content and the research on how students learn best. Most teachers, for example, don't actually know why we 'carry the 1' in addition problems or why one graphing function is appropriate and another is not." Teachers hold onto a wide range of sacred cows, Kate says, particularly when it comes to teaching literacy, about how students learn to read and write. Those less-than-best practices come from how teachers "learned to read and love to read and the books and stories that we feel are important." For these teachers, relying on the same old textbook is a security blanket that allows them to teach content without needing to deeply understand why that content is actually important or how it helps a student in the long run.

The second obstacle cited by Kate, and reinforced by several others with whom I spoke, is particularly challenging when standards are changing and teachers are expected to make those changes in real time. Finding available learning tools and using them well are two very different things. In the rush to teach to new standards, Kate says that "many teachers are just making up their own materials as they go along," and hard data seem to support her on this. The national Rand study found that most teachers create at least some of their own instructional resources. Although this is great if the teachers have a deep understanding of how to create good learning resources, Kate says that "the majority don't," and that those who are not well-versed in effective content creation are disproportionally teaching in disadvantaged schools.

Rebecca Kockler of Louisiana says that the biggest challenge of any curriculum is "coherency," the degree to which one unit of curriculum fits with another in ways that actually lead to better student understanding. Much of what is available in the OER marketplace, says Rebecca, "is still in bits and pieces." As teachers search for materials that conform to new standards and begin to look past the publishing oligarchy, they run the risk of patching together a puzzle of content of questionable value. The Rand study found that the top three sources of content for K–8 math teachers were Google, Pinterest, and Teacherspayteachers.com, none of which have been subject to any vetting. Jennifer Vranek, the founder of Education First, has been working on standards and curriculum development for 20 years and says that OER is a great opportunity, but she also says that it feeds into a K–12 system in the United States that is "incoherent relative to other highly performing countries. We are not training our educators how to judge quality or effectiveness on their own," says Jennifer. "Teachers grab something off of the Internet because they need it for class tomorrow. It might not be an effective tool, and may actually be contrary to what we know is most effective for student learning. We need vastly better quality control before we can be confident that OER meet [their] potential."

As teachers search for materials that conform to new standards, and begin to look past the publishing oligarchy, they run the risk of patching together a puzzle of content of questionable value.

The Huge Benefits of OER

The most obvious benefit of OER is simple: These materials are cheaper than traditional textbooks, and budget-pinched schools should be looking for every possible way to shift resources to critical needs. A study of the cost of middle and high school science materials (Wiley et al., 2012) found that "the average *annual* cost of a traditional textbook was $11.43. This figure represents the cost of the textbook amortized over the seven-year replacement cycle. The average cost of an open textbook was $5.14. This represents a savings of $6.29 per student per course per year. If a district of 10,000 students adopted open textbooks for its four science courses (earth science, biology, chemistry, and physics) over a seven-year adoption period, the savings would amount to $62,000 × 4 course × 7 years, or $1,761,200." Another report published (2016) by TJ Bliss when he was at the Idaho State Department of Education and by Susan Patrick of the International Association for K–12 Online Learning (iNACOL) looked at the positive fiscal impact of OER if the state of Washington adopted even a small volume of OER. They calculated that "if just one open textbook in each grade (9–12) were developed and adopted next year, the state of Washington would save an estimated $6 million, even accounting for textbook adoption cycles."

By definition OER are digital, so they can be updated much more frequently than printed books, and digital materials allow interaction with students and teachers. As digital materials replace printed books, we are closing in on the last days when students are forbidden to mark up their text. OER directly supports a deeper learning model that is more personalized, engaging, creative, and adaptable. And gone are the days when students and teachers have to use books until the end of the normal replacement cycle, even if, or when, those materials are found to include errors or omissions.

OER have started to break the stranglehold on K–12 content that has evolved into a publisher-controlled oligarchy. In addition to the states that are developing their own OER programs, there is a growing OER industry, much of it among not-for-profits that supply OER to the K–12 market. In *#EdJourney* I wrote about the CK–12 Foundation, cofounded by Neeru Khosla and her spouse, Oracle founder, Vinand. Their library of traditional content and newer animated and video resources continues to grow, as well as the ability to take any pieces from the library and customize a more traditional-looking textbook at a fraction of publisher costs. Edutopia's guide to OER in 2013 leads to a trove of other free sources: Project Gutenberg, Big History, Curriki, the OER Commons, MIT Open Courseware, and more. Rebecca Kockler believes that this increased field of content providers will have a powerful long-term impact on the quality of education. "The biggest power of OER is transparency," says Rebecca. "If you say something is good for kids, it really should be. OER allow people to ask the quality question; it has pushed the envelope on real quality of the material we use in the classroom."

In the long term, perhaps the most important benefit of OER is that it allows and empowers teachers and students to act as co-owners, not recipients, of the learning process. This empowerment is one reason why the forward-looking Hewlett Foundation has made OER a major pillar of its funding priorities for the transformation to deeper learning in education. TJ Bliss, who oversees OER issues with the Hewlett Foundation, says that OER use is still limited but growing among districts that see the potential to advance the deeper learning model. "Think about if your district had adopted OER prior to the roll-out of new, higher standards," says TJ. "Rather than waiting to see what the publishers delivered, a district could have paid their *own* teachers to develop existing OER resources to meet the new standards. Those educators would have been completely empowered in the process rather than worried about what was coming and how to implement it. Isn't that what we want our educators to be invested in?"

> *In the long term, perhaps the most important benefit of OER is that it allows and empowers teachers and students to act as co-owners, not recipients, of the learning process.*

Back to Wolfram Alpha: The (Kind of Scary?) Future of Open Knowledge

If district offices, state legislatures, and some parents are still squeamish about giving students and teachers access to free, high-quality content that actually looks and acts *somewhat* like a familiar textbook, the next generation of OER is already here . . . and will make the squeamish seasick while the courageous root for more.

As I mentioned in the introduction to this chapter, if there is a peek into the future of open access to knowledge, it is the website Wolfram Alpha. I had not heard of Wolfram Alpha until January 2016, and there are still many educators for whom that strange name is still a mystery. It probably won't be much longer. Wolfram Alpha represents just one step in the quantum leap that is going to make the "instructional manual" form of content delivery obsolete.

The site was developed by Stephen Wolfram, a British scientist who is generally accepted as one of the smartest people on the planet. At age 12 he wrote a dictionary of physics; he got his PhD at Cal Tech in particle physics when he was 20. His company Wolfram Research owns and sells Mathematica, which for 25 years has been a major system and language of technical computing. I happened to be using the example of Wolfram Alpha as an indicator of radical changes in the learning environment at a school workshop near Baltimore when an attendee raised his hand and said "I helped launch the site." Needless to say, the next week I was interviewing Josh Jones-Dilworth, a young marketing and product developer.

Josh says Wolfram Alpha does a couple of things that are beyond anything else that humans have had access to up to this point. "It's a step in the larger staircase towards truly computable knowledge. It essentially asks the question 'What if you had all of the factual knowledge in the world in one place?'" It allows a user, for free, to ask complex questions; Josh uses the example of a simple but obtuse question such as "What age will President Obama be at the next full moon?" There is no database or page on the Internet that already has this answer; it requires a computation that takes into account the president's birthday and the date of the next full moon. Wolfram Alpha grabs everything it can find in the public domain that can be represented as one or more data points and does some basic math. It brings together huge data sets, many of which are available to everyone, and some that are less accessible, and gets them to work together in ways that enable these computations to take place. To a non-technology person like me, it is frighteningly complex and remarkably simple at the same time.

What grabbed my attention when I first saw Wolfram Alpha was that it not only returns answers across an enormous range of subject areas but also, for objective problems in areas such as math, chemistry, and physics, it shows the user the *steps to how* the problem is solved. Josh says this is because "it is essentially a calculator, or what a calculator would be if it graduated from college and went to grad school and did a postdoc and got trained by a whole bunch of really smart professors. A Google search just shows you the answer, not how it got there." Wolfram Alpha represents a competing philosophy toward access to knowledge, the difference between a "black box" answer and one that is vastly more complex, but open source.

Is Wolfram Alpha a bright glimpse into one future of learning? Josh thinks that tools such as these free us up to deal with problems that are not easily computable. It represents what he calls "virtuous cooperation" between machines and people. "Humans are best suited to creating things like Wolfram Alpha, and Wolfram Alpha is best suited to doing large computations quickly. The educator's role should be to teach humans to use their higher-end cognitive abilities, because the rest is already the purview of machines." It seems hard to argue that teachers who want to block students from accessing sites such as Wolfram Alpha are merely playing the little Dutch boy against an inevitable North Sea of free, valid, and useful knowledge. Don't we all want our students to have access to the knowledge and engines of the future, not just those of the past?

How We Will Press This Lever

If there is any sector of society that should take the lead in opening access to knowledge, it is education. The idea that in the 21st century access to knowledge by child learners is a multibillion-dollar-a-year for-profit industry is just wrong. I am not a communist; I understand the workings of markets and that in most sectors of the economy it is money and profit motive that drive the creation of commodities such as textbooks. But in the area of education, we have to change the market forces. Knowledge is and should be free, and now we have the technology to make it so. We can enable this fundamental shift in how learners and knowledge intersect, if we just have the will.

In 2016, the collective of large OER providers served about 6% to 7% of the US PK–12 content market, according to Larry Singer. He thinks that within two to three years this will jump to about 25%, with the major publishers splitting the remainder among themselves. OER organizations will increasingly market to district decision makers at the same time that individual teachers will increasingly develop the skills of how to find, access, and use a much wider range of content with their students. We are on a steeply rising curve of open content access, so pressing this lever is running with, not against, that tide.

Getting Started

- Research the actual laws and regulations under which your school operates that control purchase of teaching materials. Find out if teachers *are required* to use a certain book, or if that is just tradition that has become locked in place. Ask questions!
- Set a school or district-wide goal to sunset traditional textbooks over a certain number of years. My suggestion is to set a target of reducing traditional textbook purchases by at least 50% over the next four to five years.
- Begin to turn your teachers and students from *consumers* of published material into *creators, curators, sharers,* and *evolvers* of knowledge. Implement sustainable incentives for teachers to create their own curriculum and resource materials. Shift money from the budget for book purchases to a professional development account and stipend teachers to build curriculum and materials over the summer. They will love the extra income, your school or district will save money, and teachers will have vastly more ownership in what they are teaching.
- Form partnerships with some of the major OER providers that I have mentioned in this chapter or others. Find out what they have to offer that aligns with you and your school's learning goals. Use them to help you calculate and present potential cost savings to site or district leadership as you shift to more use of OER. Connect teachers with user groups of other teachers through these OER providers so they can learn and share the skills of resource creation and the products that they create.
- Showcase student projects and work that are made possible through the use of rapidly updatable and hyperlinked digital resources that would not be possible using traditional textbooks.

Taking It to the Next Level

- Form a close relationship between K–12 schools and schools of education in your region. Lobby to increase training of teachers in how to create resource materials, develop pedagogy, and pilot new instructional practices. If you are a college-level educator or administrator, lead a design team at your college to map a plan to incorporate use of OER into your credentialing program for K–12 teachers.

- Lobby your state and district offices to ensure that the savings from a shift to OER do not get lost in the general fund, where they will be gobbled up by whatever is currently the most pressing need. These savings should be repurposed into two areas: quality control of OER and teacher professional development specifically focused on the creation, compilation, and use of OER within a deeper learning pedagogy.
- Rebuild learning processes in the classroom *around* open resources, not *in spite of* them. Yes, this means we have to rethink and redesign the nature of quizzes and homework, but the preponderance of actual evidence proves that these tools are either marginally or completely ineffective in terms of long-term learning. Our students need to know how to use open resource tools such as these in the future; they don't have to know all of the content the tools contain.
- Create a citywide or regional team of classroom educators to share how to adjust instructional practices to take advantage of the power of OER. Empower the team to offer EdCamp–style meet-ups, open to all teachers in the district or city to share best practices in how to create and use OER.

In 25 years we will look back and it will only be in the dim memory of a few senior teachers and now-young students that in 2016 we were stumbling over how to build learning on the use of open resources. Knowledge will be agnostically available and accessible. Districts will have redirected money that was wasted on outdated textbooks to ongoing professional growth for their teachers. The only question is whether or not you and your school or district will be running with this tide or sitting, like King Canut, watching it roll inexorably in.

CHAPTER FIVE

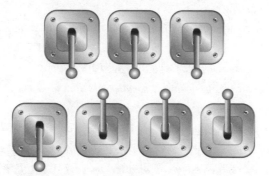

Lever #4
Fix How We Measure Student Success and Admit Students to College

Everybody knows the system is irrational, that the system is out of whack.
Richard Weissbourd, lead author of "Turning the Tide"

I never tell my students what they need to do to get an A.
Tina Seelig, Stanford University

Average is officially over.
Thomas Friedman, *Thank You for Being Late*

Like many other teenaged best friends, Anya and Emmy can complete each other's sentences. Anya does more of the talking, but Emmy is every bit the deep thinker. I wanted to hear students' perspectives on high school student assessments and the college admissions grind, and these two bright, driven juniors at Mt. Vernon Presbyterian High School in Atlanta are uniquely qualified to speak to the problems and potential solutions. When they were just sophomores they took a hard look at their routes to college, did not like the menu of traditional choices, and decided to do something about it. Specifically, they did not want to choose between what they saw as shallow, rigid Advanced Placement courses that they knew were important to colleges admissions officers and what they actually were interested in learning.

So, with the audacity of youth and support from their school, they wrote their own AP course, submitted it to the College Board, and in 2015–2016 took their own class, the first ever student-written and approved AP course. It was an extraordinary journey through literature, philosophy, social evolution, and the nature of learning, driven by their mutual interests and mentored by an informal support team of inter-disciplinary teachers and outside advisors. They told me that what drove them to take on this project was the fact that "schools don't measure what we say we value, and that is directly linked to the college application process. We talk to college reps and they tell us what they are looking for and it is not related at all to doing well on stan-dardized tests. But then they want to see all of those AP courses and straight As on our transcripts. College applications are stressful and tiresome and they don't showcase what the colleges say they are looking for. Colleges and K–12 need to work together to fix this and it does not seem all that hard."

We don't need any more research to tell us that our combined system of student assessments and college admissions are messed up, overstressing our young people, and working against any kind of meaningful school transformation. Just ask the kids.

There is an enormous, rigid dam that stresses students, constrains and frustrates teachers, frightens parents, and kills innovation at most schools: college admissions. At school after school, district after district, I hear a variation on the same anxious theme: "We can be innovative in elementary and middle schools, but our parents are afraid of changes in the high school because it might jeopardize their kids' chances at college admissions." The twin blocks in this dam, how colleges admit students and how college admissions in turn drive K–12 student assessment, par-ticularly in high school, are *the* biggest obstacles to innovation in schools. We, the community of school stakeholders, have been complicit in erect-ing and preserving these blocks, and we have total control over them. We built the dam, we preserve the dam, and we can bust it wide open with no permission from anyone and no threat other than to our own fear of change. The dam is rotten to its core, needing just a stick or two of well-placed dynamite to breach it forever. Why? Because just about everyone—educators, parents, students, college professors, university presidents and admissions officers, and employers—agrees that the system is wrong and is only getting worse.

Why this evil twin system of student assessment and college admissions is wrong is so well documented that I won't reprise the detailed arguments here. I will touch on a few highlights and quote a tenth of the voices and cite a tenth of the sources I might among the nearly universal condemnation of unequal, wrong-headed, statistically invalid grade- and test-based student assessment and college admissions. Fortunately, we are starting to see some real cracks in the dam, so most of the chapter will explore those cracks and then propose how we might blow them wide open.

We Don't Measure What We Value

Todd Rose, in his must-read book *The End of Average,* traces the twisted history and failed promises of educational and workplace evaluations, including the rise and erroneous uses of grades and standardized tests based on the statistical mythology that average measurements of performance accurately assess the individual. High school and college mission statements ring with lofty language about what we value in our students: integrity, character, creativity, grit, perseverance, risk-taking, community-based values, following passion. Yet in most schools, and particularly at the higher grade levels, we measure *none* of those. We reduce the key metrics of assessment to letter grades and a few tests designed decades ago that, collectively, measure none of what we claim to value most. Rose summarizes the problem: "The system pressures students to conformity: If they want to get admitted to a good college, students need to take the same classes, tests, and extracurricular activities that everyone else is taking—but do better than everyone else," while at the same time the high schools and colleges are telling them to stand out, to be a nonconformist in order to be recognized in the admissions process.

> *We reduce the key metrics of assessment to letter grades and a few tests designed decades ago that, collectively, measure none of what we claim to value most.*

What do we *really* value in our K–12 students and schools? I have asked thousands of teachers, students, administrators, and parents that very question. In 2014–2015 in conferences, workshops, informal meet-ups, and via social media, I asked these stakeholders from a wide range of schools to write or tweet just one word that best described "What you really want your school to reek of?" When I had collected several thousand responses I generated a word cloud, and the words that stand out are *passion, engagement, enthusiasm, excitement, curiosity, collaboration, community, inspiration, energy,* and *joy.* Similarly, many of us have gathered data from students, parents, teachers, and employers about the skills and attributes that are most important for future success of our students beyond high school, and we come up with lists full of words such as *persistence, confidence, resilience, patience, creativity, adaptability, courage, empathy,* and *self-control.* In all of these exercises, words that speak to purely academic success are almost invisible. And yet, despite almost universal agreement to the contrary, we continue to measure the success of our students, which largely determines who takes which class, who gets into college, and which ones, by a narrow set of grade- and test-based academic yardsticks.

We know for a fact that grades are almost useless in terms of describing how well a student has learned, let alone exhibits, the traits we say we value. In *Are You Smart Enough?* UCLA professor Alexander Astin cites studies that prove that over the last 45 years, "the number of college freshmen reporting high school grade averages of A has tripled, from 18% to 53%." In other words, A has somehow become the average grade for high school students, and a single C will doom a student from being accepted at most prestigious colleges. Grades have become a valid measure of almost nothing. Standardized tests, from those taken in third grade to the SAT and ACT college admissions exams, have been similarly condemned as flawed by too many people to cite. Anya Kamanetz exposes the broken system in detail in *The Test.* The business of testing, generating $2 billion in annual revenues to a handful of large companies, "seductively promises to reveal the essential, hidden nature of identity and destiny," Anya says. And yet the tests are completely at odds with what almost all of us claim to value. "The way much of school is organized around these tests makes little sense for young humans developmentally. Nor does it square with what the world needs," preaches Anya.

Next Generation Learning Challenges (NGLC) is just one of many organizations that is researching and openly sharing how we might better measure what we actually want and value in a student's growth and performance. Andy Calkins, deputy director of NGLC, speaking in May 2016 on an XQ America Challenge podcast, says schools need to focus on assessing a much wider range of learning indicators such as how students work together, how they approach problems critically, and how well they communicate their findings. NGLC has launched a series of research-based projects to critically analyze the definitions and measurements of success as we shift away from a largely test-centric assessment model. "The best way to help kids develop and demonstrate the kinds of cognitive skills that we have always cared about," Andy says, "is not to drill and drill on those skills but to incorporate them in a richer fabric of learning. We use the metaphor of learning to drive, where you need to learn some content knowledge, the rules of the road, how a dashboard works, and so on, but you don't really learn until you are out on the road in an experiential, authentic learning environment with a coach who is helping you apply what you learned in content knowledge land." In other words, students should be assessed at least as much on how well they can drive as on how well they can take a test about driving.

The Health of Our Children

In spring 2016 I attended a gathering of about 75 school leaders in Cleveland to discuss the formation of a consortium to redesign high school transcripts (more on this later in the chapter). After nearly two days of looking at data, thinking about obstacles and options, and testing how college admissions officers might respond to an assessment profile that was *not* based on grades and test scores, Scott Looney, the head of Cleveland's Hawken School and coleader of the project, rose to conclude. He got about two sentences into his final plea before he unsuccessfully choked back tears. "We have to stop doing this to our kids," said Scott to a hushed audience. "We just have to."

Why was Scott, a school executive, a lifelong educator and father of two, so emotional? Because we are damaging, and in some cases killing, our own children with a system that defines success within a narrow range of short-lived academic outcomes that determine if and where students go to college. This is not hyperbole; I wish it were, but the data are clear and compelling. Cognitive scientist Noam Chomsky (2015) calls it a "system of ideology and doctrines that turns what they (educators) are doing into something extremely harmful." A few percentage of our students wade through this gauntlet and are accepted at 10 to 20 colleges that have managed to label themselves "the best"; these students are deemed the "most successful." Another 30% or 40% of students are deemed at least "good" or "smart" enough to attend other four-year colleges of lesser reputation, each student knowing that they are not "good" enough to attend the "best" colleges. And then there are the rest, who have essentially been told, many for most of their young lives, that they are "below average" or worse. If these students go on to college at all, most will end up in two-year community college programs, which receive vastly fewer resource for, arguably, the students that need them the most.

In order to succeed in this system, many students drive themselves, with either help or tacit approval from parents and teachers, to unhealthy lifestyles, and some just give up, with tragic results. In *Excellent Sheep*, William Derisiewicz cites data from the 2010 National Survey of College and Universities Counseling Center Directors in which 91% of directors reported increasing numbers of students on their campuses with "severe psychological problems" tied to academic stressors. Rates of students reporting feelings of sadness, loneliness, depression, and anger, of students feeling anxious, overwhelmed, exhausted, and hopeless, ranged from 30% to 90% on a study of 139 college campuses. Data from a group of more than 14,000 students at 44 independent schools show that 1 student in 8 is depressed; 1 in 20 has an eating disorder; 1 in 9 seriously contemplated suicide over a 12-month period; and 1 in 17 had made a serious suicide attempt over a six-month period. Students are working more and sleeping less at a time when we know their physical and mental health depends on the opposite.

There are clear links between stress effects on teens and the academic pressures of high school and college admissions. A team from Cornell University looked at teens from "upwardly mobile and upper-middle class" families, who are overrepresented in those going on to attend four-year colleges (Luthar et al., 2013). They found in their own research, and in numerous other studies that reached a similar range of conclusions, that these young people suffer from, or are engaged in, increasing rates of substance abuse, systemic cheating, depression, anxiety, somatic symptoms, and other disorders. They cite studies by the National Center on Addiction and Substance Abuse at Columbia University (2012) that found that "the number one source of stress for teens is academic pressure, including pressure to do well in school and get into college."

The tragic and well-documented "suicide cluster" among affluent high school students in Palo Alto, California, starting in 2009—students who do not lack for safety, security, food, or social and familial support systems—was clearly traced back to the students feeling they were not meeting a completely unrealistic expectation of high school performance and college admissions. The railroad tracks that run through Palo Alto are now lined with chain link fencing, because the most common form of suicide among these students was throwing themselves in front of commuter trains. According to an in-depth review of this gruesome phenomenon, a student survey in 2013–2014 found that 12% of Palo Alto high school students had seriously contemplated suicide in the last year (Rosin, 2015).

The Wrong Results

High schools have become a sorting machine that determines which students get to go to college, to which colleges, and which do not. The standard, traditional high school program is not focused on deeper learning; it is about covering a batch of content, and then seeing which students retain and spit back that content most efficiently over a short period of time. The college admission process has built, fed, and sustained this model for decades, with no real evidence that grades and test scores correlate to success in college and beyond. Writing in *The Atlantic* in 2014, Derek Thompson cites data published by *The Chronicle of Higher Education* that shows that employers in most sectors value work experience and internships vastly more than they care about where a job applicant went to college, which makes sense, because an infinitesimal percentage of potential job applicants graduate from what are considered the elite colleges and universities.

Multiple studies have shown that the greatest correlation with how well students do on standardized college entrance exams, which remain the single most critical filter in college admissions, is to socioeconomic status. Research reported by the Jack Kent Cooke Foundation (Giancoloa and Kahlenberg, 2016) found that 72% of students in the country's most competitive colleges come from the top quartile of family income and that "high-achieving students from the bottom socio-economic quartile are one-third as likely to enroll in selective colleges compared to those from the top socio-economic quartile." Paul Tough, in *Helping Children Succeed,* reports that "the gap in eighth-grade reading and math test scores between low-income students and their wealthier peers hasn't shrunk at all over the past 20 years" and that "the difference between the SAT scores of wealthy and poor high school seniors has actually increased over the past 30 years, from a 90-point gap (on an 800-point scale) in the 1980s to a 125-point gap today."

The core flaw of a college admissions–centric high school assessment is that it dangles a carrot of completely *extrinsic* motivation to students and their families. Scott Looney of the Hawken School points out that "research on motivation suggests that students who operate with a high degree of *intrinsic* motivation outperform those who are motivated solely by *extrinsic* rewards of grades. Students will work for hours and hours to master their roles in a play or prepare for the weekend debates or hone their athletic skills without the use of grades or awards. Their motivation is intrinsic."

There is a fundamental disconnect between what colleges claim to want and what they value in terms of admissions applications. Virtually every high school principal and college counselor I have ever spoken with says that colleges publicly talk about wanting to admit students who exhibit creativity and resilience, who demonstrate real passion for learning and serving their communities, but in reality the most critical filters for most college applicants are grades, standardized test scores, and where a student went to high school. Jal Mehta from the Harvard Graduate School of Education says this disconnect extends across the systems of high school and college education in terms of what we want students to actually learn. In his research he sees that "high school teachers feel constrained in what they can teach because their students need to know x and y to get into

college. At the same time, col-   *There is a fundamental disconnect*
lege professors tell me that they   *between what colleges claim to*
really don't have a way to judge if   *want and what they value in terms*
students in their courses actually   *of admissions applications.*
know that material, so they start
at the beginning." Michael Horn, cofounder of the Clayton Christenson
Institute, boiled it down for researcher Julie Wilson: In our high schools,
"we have an elegant system for sorting people, not an elegant system for
learning."

Cracks in the Dam

The remedies to this inadequate, unfair, and increasingly dangerous
system are really quite simple, though thorough implementation will
take time, creativity, courage, and consistent pressure. Simply, we have to
measure what we claim to value in student learning, and we have to reward
progress and ability toward those goals when it comes to college admissions. If we press this lever hard and together, we will create fundamental
changes in our schools in the near term for three reasons: the solutions
are obvious, there is huge agreement about what we need to do, and we
are already seeing cracks in the dam with real potential to grow in the
near future.

One ray of light shone through a crack in early 2016 when about 80
colleges and university admissions officers, many representing what we
collectively refer to as "elite" or "highly selective" universities, including
Stanford and all of the Ivy League schools, published a document enti-
tled "Turning the Tide." It attracted immediate and widespread attention,
with news stories on television, in the printed press, and on social media.
The document is a manifesto that opens with, "Too often, today's culture sends young people messages that emphasize personal success rather
than concern for others and the common good. And too often the college
admission process—a process that involves admissions officers, guidance
counselors, parents, and many other stakeholders—contributes to this
problem." It lays out general guidelines for college admissions that will
"reward those who demonstrate true citizenship, deflate undue academic

performance pressure and redefine achievement in ways that create greater equity and access for economically diverse students." It calls for admissions offices to make it clear that more Advanced Placement courses and more short, shallow, résumé-padding one-day community service projects and vice presidencies of multiple school clubs will not enhance a student's chance of admittance; that admissions should favor students who demonstrate depth over coverage, the pursuit of interest and passion over "check off the box," and a commitment to larger goals than those of self-interest.

Within moments of its publication, education social media lit up and I was checking in with colleagues around the country to see what they thought. The general reaction from those closest to the problem, high school educators, was that "it sounds really great, but we have heard it before; only time will tell if admissions offices start to actually practice what they preach." And that is exactly what principal author of "Turning the Tide," Harvard's Richard Weissbourd, told me when we spoke on the phone a few weeks after the manifesto was published. Richard said there were two major issues that the signatories, grown to 120 in those few short weeks, meant to address. The first is "equitable access to lower socioeconomic students who have all the academic and intellectual strength to be successful across a wide range of colleges." The second is that for those students at the higher range of social and economic scales, who have traditional built-in advantages in the college-selection process, "to do something to reduce the rates of stress, anxiety, and even suicide that are one result of the current process." The goal of a college admissions application, he said, should be evidence of "meaningful academic and ethical engagement, not a long brag sheet."

Richard agreed that the proof will be in the pudding and that parents, students, high school educators, and the colleges themselves have a right to be skeptical. He said that many of the elite colleges (and he can speak only for Harvard from direct experience) had practiced much of what is in the manifesto in the past, but they have "not collectively been clear enough about it. What is important," Richard told me, "is that the paper is a *collective* signal that ethical engagement matters. It attracts public attention and discussion. When these things are done individually it does not penetrate" the public consciousness in ways that will ultimately change the system.

When this book is published, it will be too soon to see the real impact of "Turning the Tide," or a quasi-parallel multi-college collaborative, the Coalition for Access, Affordability, and Success, which is attempting to make the entire college-application process more equitable and less stressful, particularly for economically less advantaged students. These efforts will require many more signatories and strong, sustained support from the presidents and boards of trustees of colleges and universities so the practice becomes institutionally engrained, not a whim of admissions directors who come and go. The fact that the original signatories, although representing a broad range of American postsecondary schools, include most of what are commonly seen as the "top" colleges, gives cover to the rest to join. Although a relatively small number of colleges have been living this admissions creed for years, if not decades, this is a major crack that has the potential to propagate across and through the entire dam.

Reframing the High School Transcript

If colleges and universities are finally starting to clearly and more appropriately define the kind of student performance and character that they value, then the door is beginning to open for high schools to create a synergistic system of student assessment that measures those values. Similar to pioneering colleges that have devalued standardized tests in their admission process, there are high schools all over the country that assess student work without relying on inflated and irrelevant letter grades, class ranks, tests of short-term memory, and the number of hours a student has sat at a desk. Unfortunately, the number of schools that rely on other forms of more authentic assessment, that have colored outside of the college admissions lines, with highly successful records at college admissions for their students, are few. I hope within a relatively few years that is going to change.

One recent crack in the high school assessment dam is typified by the California Multi-Trade Partnership program, announced in 2016, which is a collaboration between the California Department of Education and the California Labor Federation. Students at more than a dozen pilot high schools throughout California can take courses that accumulate toward a certification in vocational jobs that are in high demand, while still taking a college-preparatory program of classes. After high school, graduates serve full workplace apprenticeships, and after four years they are eligible and qualified for full union jobs in a variety of trade industries that have age-ing workforces and will increasingly need skilled workers for well-paying jobs in the next 20 years. According to a national study by the National School Boards Association (2016) that tracked data from 15,000 high school students around the country, "high credentialed non-college goers earned 39 percent more than non-credentialed non-college goers, and 21 percent more than 2-year degree holders at age 26. *The high credentials group trailed the 4-year degree graduates in hourly wage by only 3.4 percent*" [my italics]. Formalizing apprenticeship and apprentice-like opportunities for high school students replicates the development of work-readiness traditions that we can trace back to Middle Age guilds and that are highly successful today in Germany and other European countries.

Another crack with true dam-busting potential is forming among a group of schools that are challenging the very paradigm of high school assessment. The Mastery Transcript Consortium of high schools has set out to reimagine, rewrite, and sell to colleges, schools, and parents a new high school transcript that is based on a more balanced yardstick of cog-nitive and affective measures of learning. The transcript will report how a student progresses in areas such as communication skills, decision mak-ing, problem-solving, research and analysis, leadership and teamwork, and global and cultural competency. The consortium's founding members are well-known independent schools that have virtually no restrictions about how they report student assessment, and as the design becomes tested, tweaked, and accepted, it will become available to every high school, pub-lic and private, in the country. In essence, the school leaders at the core of this much-needed insurgency are throwing down a gauntlet to the col-leges: accept this transcript or we are not going to point our students, whom you really want, in your direction.

The initial response from colleges has been guarded but positive. Scott Looney at Hawken said one admission officer told him, "Great, but don't send us anything we can't digest in two minutes." (That alone speaks vol-umes about how all of the hard work of high schools and their students is reduced by overworked college admissions offices that have become pressed to be "more selective" by screening and rejecting more applicants every year.) The alternative transcript will align much more closely to an admissions manifesto like "Turning the Tide" than the current system. As one school leader said who will help in the redesign, "The colleges are asking for this; they damn well better accept it when we provide what they are asking for."

How will postsecondary schools really feel about accepting students who don't have standard letter grades and test scores to show for their past work? The Cleveland Clinic and Lerner College of Medicine, a top-rated teaching hospital, opened in 2004 with a system that, according to Neil Mehta, assistant dean of education, informatics, and technology, "everyone thought would fail." They decided to "really do Dewey, to learn by doing and reflecting. We asked just one big question: how can we create doctors who will take better care of your family?" The school has no tests, no grades, no class rankings, no lectures, and is customized to each student. "From day one," says Mehta, "first-year medical students are working with patients. If they want to shadow a doctor in one area one day and another the next, they do it. They learn by doing." One of their graduates told us about his first interview for a residency program, walking into a room without a transcript that reflected any grades or exam scores to show for his five years in medical school. "Our assessment involves daily and weekly feedback from our teachers and our peers," he told us. "In a given year we probably get more than 150 individual items of feedback on our performance, and we reflect on many of those. So I walked into the interview with this huge stack of paper, which was the only real evidence I had of my work during the last five years. As soon as the interview started, one of the doctors interviewing me asked what the stack was, and I explained it to him. He says, 'so let me get this right: for five years, every day and every week you are getting review and feedback from teachers and peers that is directly related to your learning and practice in medicine?' I nodded, yes. He said 'the interview is over; you are accepted.'"

Yes, that example is about graduate-level work, but educators will know that the process and practices are just as valid in K–12. After all, from kindergarten to graduate school, the only time we really run away from this kind of authentic assessment is in high school, and that is only because of the college admissions system.

How We Will Press This Lever

Parents and students have every right to be worried that changes in their school might disadvantage them when it comes to college admissions. They only get one shot. Why should you and your school decide to experiment on *them*? It is one of the most valid and most-asked questions I hear at schools. The answer lies in your role as an educator. Most parents and students want the system to change; you have to show them that many, though not all, colleges and universities want students who can do much more than perform well on tests. Find the real facts of college admissions and opportunities for authentic assessment and start educating your community.

Getting Started

- At parent coffees, faculty meetings, or other routine events, or using a simple survey tool, ask students, parents, and teachers to respond to these questions: "What do we most value in learning? What kinds of assessment help improve real learning?" Summarize the findings and feed them back to your community. Show how your school is putting what *they* value into action.

- Share the "Turning the Tide" manifesto with parents at all grade levels and hold a parent coffee to discuss their thoughts. Summarize these and send them in an e-mail to the presidents of colleges and universities where your graduates attend.

- If you work at a college or are connected to a college or university (college counselors, high school principals, parents of college students, college alumni, student applying to colleges), send an e-mail to the president of the college urging him or her to sign on to "Turning the Tide" or adopt similar admissions guidelines of their own and ensure, through independent reviews, that the guidelines are published, embraced, and followed.

- Suggest books such as *The End of Average* (Rose, 2015) and *Are You Smart Enough?* (Astin, 2016) for summer book reads by your faculty members and hold a reader's discussion on these topics at the start of the new school year. Ask high school teachers to share key points with their students and hold discussion groups that enable students to wrestle with the findings of these books.

- Summarize some of the hard data from *Excellent Sheep* (Derisiewicz, 2014) and other sources cited in this chapter on student health trends and share those at an evening parent event. Follow the presentation with a brainstorming session using sticky notes, asking attendees to suggest ways that these health trends might be reversed while still meeting our learning goals. Use the ideas to generate options for program changes at your school that will likely be disruptive but will make a real difference in students' lives.

Taking It to the Next Level

- Research and implement options to student assessment through organizations such as Next Generation Learning Challenges or College and Work Readiness Assessment. Search on sites such as Edutopia using the key words *authentic assessment* to find out how other schools and educators are helping increase student performance through more effective assessment strategies and tools.
- Start a pilot in one class or one grade level and get input from students and teachers on which are more effective in terms of motivation and feedback to their learning. Have students collaborate with teachers on designing assessment rubrics for a class; ask them, "What kind of feedback can a teacher give her students that will be most helpful during this semester?"
- Learn more about the development of alternative high school transcripts and send e-mails to college presidents urging them to accept nonstandard forms of assessment. As these new transcripts become widely available over the next five years, run trials at your school in parallel with traditional forms of assessment. Keep track of your high school graduates, where they are accepted to college, and those colleges that are most likely to honor and value the new transcripts.

There is one more *huge* and very easy step that colleges can take that would go a long way to busting the big dam in the college admissions funnel. (I suggested this in an op-ed piece that I sent to the *New York Times* in

2015 . . . which I guess found the delete folder rather quickly.) If you work at a college or have any relationship to a college, lobby colleges and universities to publish the minimum SAT and ACT scores needed for admittance with the pledge that, if an applicant meets or exceeds those minima, *test scores will play no further role in the admissions selection process.* Each college can set its own criteria and adjust them annually, and of course minimum scores for the more selective schools will be higher than for the less selective schools. But once over that bar, high school juniors and seniors can quit wasting time and family money on prepping to take bubble tests over and over in search of an extra 10 or 20 or 100 points. Test prep companies will be out millions of dollars, and millions of students will sleep more and spend time on things that actually matter.

CHAPTER SIX

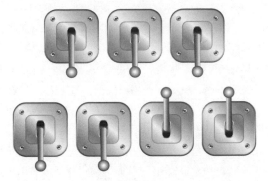

Lever #5
Teach the Teachers What They Really Need to Know

No bubble is so iridescent or floats longer than that blown by the successful teacher.

William Osler

I touch the future. I teach.

Christa McAuliffe

It takes courage and resiliency to ask for the job of principal in one of the most impoverished neighborhoods in America. It takes a powerful moral compass to stay in that job for more than a few years when other options are left begging. Although none of us wish it were so, people like Eric Juli are outliers, which is why I have tried to keep in touch with him since I first visited Design Lab Early College High School in Cleveland in 2012. Then his school occupied a dozen industrial rooms on the second story of a dilapidated building at ground zero of Cleveland's gang-ridden core. Eric spent his entire day breaking up fights, finding clothes for students who could not afford a second pair of pants, or a snack for a hungry pregnant teenager, and returning students to the classroom for discipline problems rather than kicking them out of the only semi-refuge many of them knew. The classrooms themselves seemed to be afterthoughts, closed-door traps with a tragic treaty between distrustful students and worn-out teachers: "Don't expect much from us and we won't create problems for you." He told me then, simply, "Our students don't know how to learn and our teachers don't know how to teach. That is the problem I have to solve."

In 2016 I revisited Eric and his school, still deep in the pot-holed streets of Cleveland's forgotten core, but now in their own building with a large, high-ceilinged atrium for lunch and basketball, a conference-style meeting room, a budding maker space, and a garage-quality recording studio where students can make music. Eric spends vastly less time on clothing and feeding his students, some of whom are taking classes during their senior year at Cleveland State, and others who he must kick out of school at the end of the day because they are so engaged in the music studio or the maker space. But he still gets students in ninth grade that average a fifth-grade level of reading, and the one thing that Eric says he needs to move the needle of student performance is teachers who know how to teach. He has been fighting and struggling with the system for five years and finally has a quantum group of teachers who have the desire and mind-set to actually make a difference in these kids' lives . . . if they just have the tools and skills. Eric told me he is going to put every discretionary penny he has into professional development in the next year or two. He has to break teachers out of the cycle of standing, talking, handing out worksheets, giving quizzes, and expecting that somehow the kids are going to learn, particularly with all they have stacked against them. "I just need my teachers to see what great teaching is, and these kids can make it to graduation and on to college," says Eric. And if they can do it, then so can the rest of us.

Choose your metaphor: If education is a combustion engine of learning, then teachers are the gasoline. If education is a tilled field, then teachers are the farmers. If education is a natural ecosystem and students are the plants and animals, then good teachers play a god-like role, keeping the system in balance and enabling diverse species to thrive. Any way you slice it, if you (I hope) agree that great learning gets a turbo boost in the presence of deep relationships, then teachers are a force that can drive and manage a wonderful, transformational learning experience . . . or not. So where do these critical pieces of the education system come from? How do we ensure a supply of quality teachers who are able to propel learning out of the 19th century and into the 21st? How do I, as a parent, know that my child will be trained and nurtured by a teacher who understands and can support her needs as an individual and not as one more piece on the assembly line? As I have traveled around the country visiting and working with schools for the last several years, I have heard a repeated and frustrated refrain from educators at the highest-priced private schools and the most underserved public schools: "How the heck are we supposed to transform learning for the *future* if the education colleges and universities keep training young teachers for the *past*?"

The gap between what K–12 schools need and what teachers are trained to do in our schools of education is enormous, yet there is absolutely nothing keeping us from filling that gap. This lever is just begging to be pushed. Schools of education at colleges and universities are full of bright, thoughtful, caring, aware educators who understand what the future demands, and why, and how teachers can lead that charge. Why, then, the gap? Why are colleges and universities that train teachers lagging and not leading this charge? Why do they continue to crank out the same old fuel for the industrial age when we need something bright, clean, and renewable for the information age and beyond?

Arthur Levine, the president of the Woodrow Wilson Foundation, has a résumé and understanding of education that few can equal. In 2015, the Woodrow Wilson Academy of Teaching and Learning partnered with MIT to open a new graduate program for teacher training that will enroll its first class in 2017. Arthur told me that "the condition of education and schools of education today is not surprising. We are moving from an industrial to an information economy and every social institution—government, churches, financial and labor markets, communication—is stuck in this period of transition. Education leaders at the university level don't even admit that they are broken; they defend their practice, and that is just not good enough anymore." Arthur thinks it might take a couple of generations to break graduate schools of education out of their inertia, but he and others already see the problems and how to solve them. This chapter is about how those solutions are taking root today and how it is not just the professors who can make a real difference by pressing on this lever of change.

The Legacy Problem

When most of us think about the big university or the state college across town, we might think first of the football team, the mascot, or the new science center they built last year. Graduate schools of education don't occupy the most prominent spot at most colleges. Most postsecondary schools of education have never had the status of other university graduate programs such as engineering, business, law, the physical sciences, or medicine. Although there are certainly research opportunities, education is viewed more as an applied field. Stephen Hamilton, dean of the High Tech High Graduate School of Education, says that "education schools have a perceived second-tier status as a field for fruitful research. There are not a lot of wealthy alumni who attended colleges of education, so it is hard to raise money at the college level." Add that to low pay for teachers in the workforce, and many colleges don't see schools of education as a high priority. Gayle Kolodny Cole, an ex–Teach for America teacher, now a veteran of the classroom, framed the problem bluntly, perhaps even brutally. "I went to a dinner party a couple of years ago with a group of mostly college education professors," Gayle told me, "and had three different conversations, all about the same thing: how hard it is to think about pedagogy and learning when tenure is all about publishing or obscure research. There is just not much prestige or money in college education programs in improving pedagogy." And, ironically, says, Gayle, education school is not a place where many people have a progressive or deeper learning experience themselves. "Most graduate education programs are completely antithetical to what we are saying deeper, student-centered learning needs to be."

"Most graduate education programs are completely antithetical to what we are saying deeper, student-centered learning needs to be."

Other education veterans have similarly harsh views of what drives many current schools of education. Ken Kay, CEO of EdLeader21, who has been deeply embedded in K–12 education for several decades, describes most schools of education as factories: "They are there to feed the need for young teachers." Stephen Hamilton adds that there are very real practical issues in training new teachers in an authentic learning environment: "It requires a college faculty member to go out and observe the trainees in their internships, which takes them away from time dedicated to research and publishing, which is how faculty move up on the tenure track. Often it is only the lower level or marginal college faculty member who will take the time for this kind of important supervision."

Schools of education suffer from the same level of inertia, or worse, than what we see in K–12 education. Colleges are large, complex institutions, and with tenured faculty and the lifetime positions they bring, the pace of change can be downright glacial. David Chard is the president of Wheelock College in Boston, but for years he was dean of the Annette Caldwell Simmons School of Education and Human Development at Southern Methodist University and a member of Deans for Impact, a collaboration of college education school deans who are trying to shift best practices of education schools around the country. David says that many state teacher certifications, regulations, and standards have not changed in a very long time, and he points to the enormous gap between what the certifications require and what we know about how teachers learn best. "States largely mandate," David says, "that teachers come out of education schools with a very fixed and uniform set of experiences, at the same time that K–12 education is radically differentiating the learning landscape. There is very good evidence that young teachers' best and most powerful learning comes from their experiences in the classroom," yet most universities are stuck on a student-credit or time-in-seat model of course work that is antithetical to the kind of collaborative, project-based, deeper learning that we want teachers to increasingly employ. One long-term member of an education school faculty who asked not to be named put it as bluntly as he could: "Most state schools of education are nothing more than puppy mills. They get paid to turn out teachers at a fixed rate, so we get quantity with no focus on quality."

Jal Mehta of the Harvard Graduate School of Education points out that during this period of transition from an outdated education model to a deeper learning model more attuned to what students will need in the future, the majority of K–12 schools, districts, and therefore teaching jobs are still at highly traditional schools. Jal sees change taking place, but not on all of the levels needed to truly transform the learning experience. "I think there are two kinds of potential shifts. Within a given traditional discipline, many postsecondary programs train teachers to move away from teaching rote learning to more conceptual learning. But in terms of project-based work, interdisciplinary courses, and other hallmarks of a deeper learning model, postsecondary faculty [members] are still largely focused on the old paradigm because they are organized around discipline-based silos themselves. This is understandable: They are trying to prepare teachers for the jobs there are, and most schools are still locked in a traditional model."

In Alexander Astin's frank expose of what colleges value, *Are You Smart Enough?*, he lays the blame for weak preparation of future teachers bluntly and squarely at the feet of college and university faculty who, after all, largely determine the selection of graduate students, what curriculum they will teach, program and graduation requirements, and how the teachers-in-training will be assessed in their progress. Unfortunately, teaching is not a top priority for most college professors, he writes. "Faculty members who simply want to earn the respect of their colleagues all invest an inordinate amount of time conducting research and writing papers for publication. These practices help to explain why many university professors continue to invest relatively little time in carrying out their teaching and mentoring activities."

The gulf between the teachers we need and the teachers we are preparing is visceral for educators who are desperately trying to accelerate the pace of change in our K–12 system. Ken Kay of EdLeader21 thinks there are only a handful of education schools that are truly teaching teachers to succeed in a deeper learning environment, and that the vast majority, perched in their all-too-real Ivory Towers, just don't see either the need or the urgency. "In one of the states where we have a number of district partners," Ken says, "I called two state university deans of education and offered to bring in a group of superintendents who wanted to talk about how the education schools could better prepare teachers to be successful in their districts. One dean said 'we really are not interested,' and the other said 'let me think about it' and then never got back to me."

New Models That Work

This problem screams to be fixed, and the obstacles and solutions almost all lie within the control of those who can do the fixing. There are a relatively small number of education graduate schools and teacher training programs that are active in program development and intimate partnerships with local and regional school districts. But the vast majority of teachers are trained at the roughly 1,400 teacher education schools that remain largely stuck in an outdated model. What gives me hope that this is a lever that we can, in fact, successfully press?

One example, cited by almost everyone I talked to, is that of High Tech High (HTH) Graduate School of Education in San Diego. California allows school districts to train and certify teachers, a crease in the system that HTH, a charter middle and high school, exploited in creating first a teacher certification program, and now a full graduate school of education. In what Stephen Hamilton of HTH Graduate School calls a "gutsy move," the school busted the existing model of lecture-based learning that forms the programmatic core at most graduate schools, and developed a pedagogy that mirrors how HTH teaches in their high school and middle school programs. "Unlike most colleges," says Stephen, "we don't have a faculty member standing up at the front of the room lecturing to a hall of 150 graduate students on how to 'do' project-based learning, for example. We teach using the same practices that we expect teachers to use when they go out on their own." The graduate students spend vastly more time practicing in the High Tech High and middle schools than sitting in their own classrooms. Stephen recognizes that their graduates might not be comfortable going on to teach in a more traditional K–12 setting. "There is no question there is a gap between how we want to prepare a teacher at HTH and what is expected of them at most schools and districts. But we want to prepare our graduates to play the role of change agents ready for the future, no matter where they end up."

"We want to prepare our graduates to play the role of change agents ready for the future, no matter where they end up."

Thought leader, researcher, teacher, and author Yong Zhao says that HTH Graduate School is an example of leading-edge teacher training that could have enormous long-term impact. "Students are so different now than they have been in the past; they have tremendous potential as classroom resources to support their own learning and the learning of other students. Teachers need to learn to retreat from the idea that they have to instruct in every facet. This requires some flexibility in the curriculum, but that is well within the power of many graduate school educators." He sees HTH Graduate School as an entirely new model of teacher training, in which young teachers are embedded in schools and work in cohorts to explore and then build their own practices. "We have to imagine," Yong says, "a whole new kind of graduate education program, a two-year experience of designing and practicing teaching with no course work whatsoever. The only obstacles to this kind of much more innovative, experienced-based learning are pressures from traditionally minded faculty and restrictions from the accreditation bodies, both of which are wholly within the control of educators."

Arthur Levine says that the new graduate program at MIT will be that kind of school, "something very different from the experience at most of the other 1,400-plus schools of education in the country. It will reinvent the process of teacher education around the core element of competency, not time." Arthur says that there are three critical ingredients that will differentiate the program at MIT, all of which are nearly novel in the world of graduate education, but all of which shift the program toward a deeper learning experience. First, all of the materials MIT develops and uses for instruction will be open source and available to any other training program or individual. Second, the school will be what Arthur calls "a laboratory of learning," because the school will put results of trial programs into the hands of policy makers in real time. Third, in order to breach the frustrating lack of coordination between the graduate schools and school districts, MIT will deeply partner with school districts so young teachers are helping to create a new learning ecosystem in parallel with their own education and training.

Arizona State University offers another model for disrupting the inertia of a legacy land grant teacher's college by recognizing that the future of K–12 learning will look very different from the past. Ryen Borden was executive director of the Sanford Inspire program in the School of

Education at ASU before leaving to work for the Bill and Melinda Gates Foundation. In 2014 ASU launched a five-year project to infuse project-based learning into their own teaching curriculum to ensure that teachers have these skills when they go off to their own classrooms. "The college faculty has to teach using these methods if we hope for our own student teachers to learn them and use them in the future. ASU is in year two of the project and we want to make the resources we are developing open and available so any teaching college can use them. We see a real need for these resources; a lot of teaching colleges don't have the resources to build them on their own." Similar to MIT, ASU is also breaking the model of time-based course work, developing targeted micro-courses, differentiated learning for each graduate student, credentialing, and badging within the teacher education program. Ryen cites two obvious reasons: "because it is highly effective and also so teacher candidates will have the experience of this kind of program design and authentic assessment to take with them when they go out to their own new jobs."

Many of the educators I interviewed for this chapter were optimistic that these changes would take hold at scale, though perhaps on a time line that is still frustrating for this generation of education reformers and, most important, this generation of students. Ryen said that "in 20 years there will be multiple pathways to becoming a good teacher. Some of what we are working on—micro-credentialing, competency-based programming and assessment—are really starting to gain traction in the postsecondary education community."

How We Will Press This Lever

Pressing this lever will take time and a sustained commitment, but it will radically alter the trajectory of change in the education system, similar to shifting a race car to a richer, high-octane fuel. We are simply not going to move education unless we change how K–12 schools operate, and teachers are the fuel that those schools run on. If, as Jal Mehta of Harvard says, "we train teachers, and they enter or go back into schools that don't value a deeper learning method, transformation will fizzle. The good news is that, when I go to schools and evaluate how many teachers are already trying a more innovative approach, I think it is about 20% of the teachers. That may not seem like a lot, but there are 3.5 million teachers in America, and 700,000 is a lot of teachers."

K–12 Schools Pressing the Lever

- Make a critical list of the learning conditions you want to provide for your students. Then develop laser focus in your staff development plan around the elements of great learning. Connect with groups such as the Deeper Learning Network to research professional training providers who specialize in pedagogy and instruction that is aligned with your highest aspirations of the learning experience.
- Work with your administration, union, and teacher collaboratives to develop hiring practices that prioritize training in deeper learning. Find teacher colleges that teach deeper learning practices and build connections to hire graduates from those colleges. In the hiring sequence, ask candidates to demonstrate evidence of creativity, team collaboration, dedication to personal and professional growth, and a knowledge of at least some practices of deeper learning.
- Set up a meeting with the dean of your local or regional school of education. Start building a coalition of schools that demand future-focused teacher training from these colleges. Include community business leaders in the coalition; they need a workforce that has been trained in deeper learning, not filling in bubbles on worksheets and tests. Bring representatives of this diverse group of school and business leaders to meet with the college presidents and deans. Be empathetic about the obstacles faced at the college level but collaboratively set out an agenda that will substantively change the education school curriculum over a relatively few number of years.

Colleges Pressing the Lever

Much of the responsibility for this challenge lies squarely with the faculty and administration of the education schools and with the certification committees, with whom the various state education schools have enormous influence. This is a complex web of relationships in which it is easy to say that colleges can't change until the K–12 schools demand it, and K–12 schools can't change until the colleges train teachers for the future. The solution has to be designed by a diverse group collaborating toward a common goal.

- Following the collaboration among college admissions offices that generated "Turning the Tide," the presidents of forward-leaning public and private colleges and universities that offer graduate education programs, spread around the country, should commit to transform these programs to deeper learning–centered teacher training programs within the next five years.
- College educators have to start adopting deeper learning practices themselves to get out of the lecture hall mode of instruction. Deans of schools of education should incentivize their faculty to develop and share, via open sources, training modules and materials for their own graduate programs that use and highlight deeper learning practices.
- Every college that is part of this collaboration should commit to partner individual faculty members and teachers-in-training in one or more school districts in their city or region, focusing in particular on those districts with traditionally underserved student populations. The college faculty should routinely meet with superintendents, principals, and teachers in their respective areas to understand changing needs and demands of the local schools.
- Colleges and partner districts should press heavily on state departments of education and credentialing authorities to rewrite teacher credentialing requirements with deeper learning competencies. Credentialing authorities should *lead* toward the future and require that schools of education require some tracks, as options at a minimum, that focus on the pedagogy, curriculum, and instruction of deeper learning.

As Arthur Levine noted, there are two alternatives for the kinds of transitions that education is facing: You can either *replace* or *repair* what no longer works. Generally, Arthur believes, "the for-profit world replaces and the not-for-profit world repairs." If education schools are going to be part of the solution for this generation of students, or the next, the reparations need to be bolder, faster, and more intentional than they are right now. It will take time for this model to take over as a dominant paradigm in graduate education programs, and in the meantime, says Arthur, "we have to repair at least some of the existing education schools or we risk losing another two generations of young teaching students."

CHAPTER SEVEN

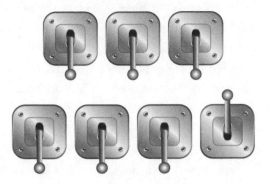

Lever #6
Connect, Flow, and Rethink "School"

You never change things by fighting the existing reality. To change something,
build a new model that makes the existing model obsolete.

Buckminster Fuller

To enhance stability in rapids it's important to move as fast or faster than the
current. Every time you . . . drag your paddle . . . makes you more vulnerable
to flipping over.

Anna Levesque, whitewater kayaker, *Thank You for Being Late*

I eyed Ozan warily across a dimly lit room, picking my way carefully through a maze of
furniture. I gingerly selected a large red block, and set it on a long wooden table that
filled half of the room. I carefully stacked a blue block on top of the red one, staring down
at my hands as if they belonged to some slightly fractal alien or a clown with four fingers
and the motor skills of a baby. Ozan handed me what looked like a Nerf blaster loaded
with yellow balls, but I dropped it; clumsy me. We tossed a basketball back and forth
a few times, though the forces of gravity seemed to have been ever so slightly twisted.
I followed Ozan outside to the back patio, to a sunny afternoon and a lawn filled with

Frisbees and yard furniture, and a large white projector screen . . . except I couldn't see the projector. Ozan started fidgeting his hands in mid-air as if molding an invisible ball of clay and a few seconds later a website appeared on the screen. I moved to get closer and stubbed my toe against a wall that wasn't there. I tried to back away, which is hard to do when you are up against something that is not there, and turned to make sure there was nothing behind me that was also not there . . . at which point the balance in my inner ear took a hesitant detour and I had the dizzy feeling that my feet were not actually connected to the rest of me.

This was my first real experience in a powerful headset-enabled 3D virtual reality environment. Everything from the balls and blocks to the fake gravity, the long wooden table that at one point uncomfortably bisected my body, the interactive web screen, the random people sprinting past the wall outside the back yard—all were bits of code convincing my eyes and ears to create an enveloping world that comes close to the real thing. Ozan was real but he was not in the room with me; he could have been on the other side of the world. When he was right next to me in this digital universe I could converse with him, just as if we were talking in a quiet classroom or bar; when he moved away his voice faded. When I dropped a ball it fell to the ground, and when I tossed a ball or a block they rose and fell along arcs described by real-world Newtonian physics. With a little training and some different bits of the open source code that High Fidelity is using to create these virtual reality environments, we could have built a robot, designed a building, or dissected a frog together. As it was, a moment after we were in the digital backyard we jumped to St. Mark's Square in Venice, where I wanted to meet a professor of Renaissance art, and a moment after that we were inside a human tissue cell, where I wanted to meet a research biologist.

By the time anyone reads this, everything I saw and experienced in those ten minutes in spring 2016 will be old hat, trumped by something way more advanced, likely powered by the phone in your pocket, that will make the laptop I am using to write these words seem as obsolete as the 30-pound Royal typewriter that my father kept in the den when I was a child.

This chapter is different from the others because this lever is being forged right now. We don't know exactly what it will look like or how it will work in "schools" of the future, but, like rails in front of a train, we can see where the path leads. Some of this chapter will feel exciting; much of it might be uncomfortable because the future is almost always a combination of opportunity and fear.

How we connect as humans, the most fundamental term of the learning equation, is undergoing a process of revolutionary change. We must understand this change, embrace it, and make sure the new educational tools that will soon be at our command are powerfully aligned to great learning, not frittered away. This chapter is also the longest in the book because it brings together several evolving threads that cannot be separated: the impacts of true digital transformation, the keys to creative innovation, an explosion of new technological opportunities for our teachers and students . . . and a world of education that has just a glimmer right now of how to handle all of that. Strap in, be courageous, and get ready to flow. As we will see, *flow* is a very big deal.

Change *Requires* Connectivity

Let's start with two hard facts: *innovators lead innovation,* and *K–12 education does a remarkably poor job of incubating innovators.* One of the black letter laws of organizational change, gleaned from about 500 years of post-Renaissance organizational evolution, is that *connectivity*—from the coffee shops frequented by Venetian spice traders, to Thomas Edison's New Jersey labs, to bars and mash-ups in Silicon Valley—empowers innovation. We don't innovate on our own, sitting and thinking with feet up on a desk. We try, meet, share, dream, fail, iterate, try again, and fail again *with others.* Noted psychologist Mihaly Csikszentmihalyi (1990) links this kind of connectivity to something vastly more fundamental and intrinsically motivating than business success: happiness. His research suggests that people are actually happier when they experience a state of flow, which he describes as "an optimal state of intrinsic motivation." It is in linking to other people who are fully and passionately engaged in what they are doing that we find the collective power of connectivity, and it is through connectivity that people and organizations grow and change.

> *It is in linking to other people who are fully and passionately engaged in what they are doing that we find the collective power of connectivity, and it is through connectivity that people and organizations grow and change.*

Walter Issacson, in *The Innovators,* his expansive book on the roots and growth of the digital age that has reframed much of the human experience, says that the keys to this remarkable revolution lay in the combination and connection of wildly diverse people and perspectives, "the product of a research ecosystem that was nurtured by government spending and managed by a military-industrial-academic collaboration. Intersecting with that was a loose alliance of community organizers, communal-minded hippies, do-it-yourself hobbyists, and homebrew hackers, most of whom were suspicious of centralized authority."

Growing out of this brew over the last 40 years, Silicon Valley and sister innovation hubs all over the world have developed an extraordinary density of talent and passion for the technology revolution. That density enabled a "Valley model" to form that empowers flow over industrial age rigidity: frequent formal and informal connections, mobility of workers between companies, and an openness and sharing of ideas among people who might compete in the workplace and also be close friends. Dean of the University of California, Berkeley, School of Information, Anna Lee Saxenian, uses the word *recombitorial* to describe how people move from company to company and how companies constantly form and re-form along with the ebb and flow of ideas, success, failure, and recombustion. These movements create an ever-roiling stew of creativity as groups find new ways to merge ideas at their margins, which have always held the greatest potential for innovation. In his book *Creativity, Inc.*, an absolute must-read for educators, Edwin Catmul, cofounder of Pixar, one of the most successful companies in the world, says that *how* they view connectivity lies at the very core of their success. "Too many of us think of ideas as being singular, as if they float in the ether, fully formed and independent of the people who wrestle with them," writes Catmul. "Ideas, though, are not singular. They are forged through the tens of thousands of decisions, often made by dozens of people," that lead to creative and sustainable change.

Finding, nurturing, growing, and supporting passionate change agents are the fundamental drivers that create actual change in organizations such as schools. Deborah Frieze is an ex-techie-turned-change provocateur. In her TEDx Talk, Frieze says that as traditional systems begin to peak, "walkouts," those courageous pioneers and sometimes quirky early adopters, start to experiment with alternatives that have little resemblance to the old systems. "If these walkouts remain isolated from one another, nothing happens," says Deborah. "The dominant system will rush, absorb, or co-opt the pioneers because every living system is inclined toward self-preservation. If they get connected to one another, exchanging information and learning, then their separate efforts can suddenly emerge as a powerful system capable of disrupting the old order and giving birth to something new."

To change the *whole* system of education, as opposed to those one-off bright lights of innovation that we see in so many schools and that I chronicled in *#EdJourney*, requires a *systemic* restructuring. According to Frieze this happens when the "trailblazers, those who have ventured outside of the system, connect and mutually support each other. This provides opportunities for 'illuminators' to show people that what is evolving is not normal, that it is a very different way of 'being.'" When a school or district supports walkouts and trailblazers in becoming illuminators to others in the system, real changes start to snowball.

When a school or district supports walkouts and trailblazers in becoming illuminators to others in the system, real changes start to snowball.

The Nurture of Networks

Schools are physically pervasive in our society, but the walkouts and trailblazers often lack the densities of connection that we find in innovative organizations. Educators are open and sharing of our ideas . . . when we happen to interact. Schools don't have a Silicon Valley packed with energetic start-ups and bars or a few Venetian coffee shops where all the traders used to hang out. We work close by each other, but few of us connect frequently beyond the silos of our classroom, office, department, grade level, or campus. There are many, many educators and schools, but we often lack *effective density* in terms of the critical connections that lead to real innovation. If there is one thing that will break the inertia that has plagued education for decades, it is frequent, rich, dense connections among the millions of adults and students for whom learning is so critically important, who have great ideas and successes to share, but who currently exist in relative isolation.

That density and frequency of professional and social connections among *all* educational stakeholders, including parents, employers, and business owners, is just now starting to emerge. We have seen an explosive rise in informal networks of educators who collaborate on their own time, with no direction from supervisors. When a few years ago teachers had no point source for informal collaboration, there are now hundreds of weekly Twitter chats, organized by and for educators, and focused around a complex matrix of "tribe," geography, and interest group. No-cost EdCamps have sprouted up in many cities and regions around the country, usually attended by teachers on a valuable weekend day, and "run" by those who show up. The blogosphere, a free-wheeling virtual bazaar for educator sharing, did not exist a decade ago.

Formal networks of schools that hold common affinities toward school change freely share what they know and learn with member schools and, increasingly, with everyone else. Chris Jackson is with one of those networks, Big Picture Learning, a rapidly growing consortium that is part of an even larger affinity group, the Deeper Learning Network. Chris says that we are "probably very close to the tipping point" where the collaborative density of connections among educators will conflagrate individual bright points of innovation into an unstoppable transformation. The public, Chris believes, has finally become more aware that there are real consequences to *not* changing the nature of education, of ignoring the message. "It is not one point source; it is a collective set of voices that is starting to shift the discussion much more dramatically than where it was a decade ago," says Chris.

These growing formal and informal networks act as templates and examples of what is possible and provide resources so everyone is not reinventing the same wheel. Access to successful examples of schools with similar challenges empowers local change agents to overcome the inevitable obstacles to change. "Large school districts often have a nontraditional school, an experimental school, often a place where lower-performing students go or

Access to successful examples of schools with similar challenges empowers local change agents to overcome the inevitable obstacles to change.

that is viewed as 'those crazy guys trying new stuff,'" says Chris, but they are often the hotbeds of real, creative innovation. "Policy leaders sometimes sort of ignore what is going on at these schools, and the educators can transform a segment of the system without direct support of, or interference from, governing bodies."

Crossing Curves

As I cited from Arthur Levine in Chapter Six, every major human institution is undergoing a fundamental response to post–industrial age reordering, and education is no exception. Consider that one generation of K–12 ago, about 13 years, when students graduating high school in 2016 were entering kindergarten, we were exploring what we thought was a dramatic new era of educational technology. Each student might have spent a few hours a week in a computer lab or shared a desktop computer with a young partner right in her own classroom. One of the major goals was for students to learn the critical skill of keyboarding during their primary grades. That's right: *The bold frontier of educational technology just one generation ago was digital typewriting.*

A half generation ago, when the graduating class of 2016 was in middle school, they were making movies on laptops, and a few were allowed to play with the first generation of the revolutionary iPad. "Distractions" such as Facebook, Twitter, and Snapchat were still largely in the future. Four years ago, when the graduating class of 2016 entered high school, one elementary class I visited had just made crude, colorful, creative toothbrushes on their first-generation 3D printer, and object-oriented programming was just starting to become common in primary grades.

In 2016 those *high school* students whom we taught to keyboard in their own primary school years were preparing to graduate and move on to college or the workplace. Here is what *elementary* school students were doing in just a few schools I visited the same year:

- Designing and building custom-fit prosthetic hands that cost less than $300, to be donated to other children who, a few years ago, would have waited in long lines to receive expensive prosthetics through their health provider, if they were lucky

- Building a paper-and-cardboard town on the classroom floor, and then programming mini-bots to navigate around the streets and into driveways
- Learning the basics of electricity by playing music on vegetables wired to a programmable amplifier and sound system
- Recording interviews on their iPhones to upload to a project file, which was then shared with their teacher, and ultimately became part of their digital portfolio for performance assessment
- Writing blogs that were read by students in other countries, launching an international student-to-student dialogue
- Creating augmented reality topographic models in a sandbox

In *one generation,* our elementary learning goals have had to shift from how to type on a keyboard to how to use computer-aided design software and program a sophisticated, industrial-grade machine to build a prosthetic hand. That, friends, is a *very* steep change curve, and it is the steepness of this curve that demands that we fundamentally change our concept of "school." In his most recent book, *Thank You for Being Late,* international thought leader and translator of global trends Thomas Friedman summarizes how the decade from 2007 to 2016 birthed and grew a matrix of major technological innovations that have created what he calls a "supernova" effect of transformation across virtually all aspects of human society. He cites his conversation with Eric "Astro" Teller, CEO of the Google X research and development lab, who explains that in the past humans have been able to keep up with major advances in technology: the wheel, the printing press, electricity, the telegraph, and the like. Teller believes we are now at a unique point in human evolution, where the ever-steepening rate of change has exceeded human ability to adapt. We simply cannot keep up with the change in the world around us. Changes in how we live our everyday lives that, in past generations, took centuries or decades to evolve, such as printing, ocean travel, the use of metals, or agrarian

In one generation, our elementary learning goals have had to shift from how to type on a keyboard to how to use computer-aided design software and program a sophisticated, industrial-grade machine to build a prosthetic hand.

practices, now evolve in years or even months: in communication, social interaction, medicine, transportation, and commerce. "The only adequate response," says Teller, "is that we try to increase our society's ability to adapt. We must rewire our societal tools and institutions so that they will enable us to keep pace. Enhancing humanity's adaptability," argued Teller, "is 90% about optimizing for learning." That is an enormous and daunting challenge for educators: *the ability of the human species to adapt to what we have the capacity to invent is 90% up to us.*

Welcome to the Cognitosphere: A System of Structured Flow

Our capacity as a species to learn, share, and adapt *is* evolving to meet this daunting challenge. In the roughly 4.5 billion–year history of the planet, there have only been four completely global, interconnected spheres: the *atmosphere* (all of the gases that surround the planet), the *hydrosphere* (water), the *lithosphere* (all of the rocks and solid parts), and the *biosphere* (organic things). In 2012 I coined the term the *cognitosphere,* what others have termed the *metaverse,* to describe the fifth global sphere, the just-now-evolving global socio-neural network of knowledge acquisition, sharing, management, and archive that is rapidly becoming accessible to anyone on the planet with an Internet-connected device. The cognitosphere is in its infancy. It did not exist 15 years ago, and it is already a dominant force in human interactions. It is the greatest tool for human connectivity and the sharing of knowledge in the history of the world . . . and education and innovation rely on knowledge and connections.

There is a surge of understanding of how the cognitosphere works, how it is structured, and what makes it the inevitable backbone of learning in the future. In a series of discussions in 2013 with Adrian Bejan, author of *Design in Nature* and one of the world's leading experts in fluid dynamics, I learned how his decades of research and mathematical modeling prove that all types of complex systems follow a set of

We know what the structure of global education will look like in the future.

principles that govern how the systems handle flow. Whether it is blood in our body, sap in trees, water in rivers, cars on freeways, or people walking around in a hospital, these systems arrange themselves in branch-like structures that maximize the efficiency of flow. Bejan confirmed for me that an evolving system such as the cognitosphere, which, for the first time in history allows for the largely unfettered flow of ideas and knowledge, will follow the same principles. That is a powerful statement: We know what the structure of global education will look like in the future.

Why is this structure important to educators? In the same way that flow is the state of optimal intrinsic motivation and has become the life force of innovation in Silicon Valley, students, teachers, and schools that help form the main branches and nodes in this kind of system will have vastly more access to, and influence on, those ideas and knowledge, than players that exist out in the small capillaries. Simply, big rivers are more important than small streams, and at some point, if a school is not close enough to the main arteries of flow, it will cease to be relevant to its learners. If schools "get into the flow," no matter where they are physically located or what their base of resources is, they can be relevant and influential in the cognitosphere.

Alex Pentland is one of the best-known scientists in the world, with connections from MIT to the World Economic Forum and beyond. In another must-read-for-educators book, *Social Physics,* Pentland reports on an extraordinary body of work "that describes reliable, mathematical connections between information and idea flow on the one hand and people's behavior on the other." Pentland and his research team gave special smartphones to groups of people and then recorded terabytes of data on how these individuals and groups acted, learned, and performed over a period of as long as a year. They found that the social interactions, in formal and highly informal settings, correlated with group performance more than how many smart individuals were on the team or how any one individual performed on a set of tasks. "The key insights obtained with social physics," says Pentland, "all have to do with the flow of ideas between people. As the pattern of connections between learners become optimal, the performance of the entire crowd improves dramatically." What was most important in terms of human group performance, they found, were the dynamic, interactive connections among members of any group, such as a class of students, not the individual performance of any one member.

The concept of flow is central to how and why learning is fundamentally changing. In *Thank You for Being Late,* Thomas Freidman cites works by John Hagel III, John Seeley Brown, and Lang Davison that suggest that we have already reached a point where *what* a person or organization *has* is being superseded by *how well they participate* in flow. Writing in the *Harvard Business Review,* Hagel, Seeley Brown, and Davison say that in the past "if you knew something valuable, something nobody else could access, you had, in effect, a license to print money. All you needed to do was protect and defend that knowledge." Now, they believe, "there's a good reason to think that value is shifting from knowledge *stocks* to knowledge *flows* [my italics]. As the world speeds up, stocks of knowledge depreciate at a faster rate," and to succeed, individuals and organizations will "have to continually refresh our stocks of knowledge by participating in relevant flows of new knowledge."

Friedman, looking at a world challenged by the crossing curves of innovation and human adaptive capacity, shifting markets, and global geopolitical realignments, says that "digital rivers (of information) now run everywhere with equal energy. So it isn't complicated: the most educated people who plug into the most flows and enjoy the best governance and infrastructure win." As the influence of these flows continue to accelerate, connections with "strangers" who first found each other through social media will mold our relationships in education, finance, communication, and mass culture. Those individuals, organizations, and societies "most open to flows" and "most willing to learn from them, and contribute to them, are the ones most likely to thrive . . . those that can't will struggle."

Great Learning Is Relational

Although we have a rapidly evolving cognitosphere for creating and sharing ideas and knowledge that was beyond our own wildest imaginations a decade or two ago, learning is about much more than just *access* to content. Ask a group of students, parents, teachers—pretty much anyone—to think about a time in their lives when they learned something so deeply that they still remember that moment of learning and the powerful lesson today. Ask them to describe that moment in a single word. I have asked thousands of people to engage in this simple three-minute exercise (that I stole from Bo Adams, who probably borrowed it from someone else!) and have recorded the words and phrases that describe those conditions of great learning. The words are not surprising because we all share these moments of great learning in our lives: supportive, friendly, coach, caring, allows risk, passion, interest, deep, collaborative, meaningful, loving, open, curious, comfortable, connected, inspiring, exciting, empathetic, inquisitive, energetic, positive, and empowered.

Learning is *relational* and *transactional,* and virtually every educator agrees that, of these, the relational is by far the more powerful. Education is fundamentally sculpted and enhanced by the nature of human interactions. Yes, we "acquire" knowledge in a transaction between the learner on the one hand and a teacher, book, computer, movie, or experience on the other. But our best and deepest learning is a function of the complex fabric that weaves together the learner and the learning experience, in which the student develops an actual relationship to the sources of knowledge and the experience of acquiring knowledge and wisdom. It is why so many of us remember specific teachers or coaches who positively affected our lives. Those words we all use to describe the conditions of great learning, the kind of learning we want for our own students and children, describe a set of relationships, not a mere transfer of knowledge or information. With deep relationships the transactions of learning become more profound; the opposite is not the case.

> *Learning is* **relational** *and* **transactional,** *and virtually every educator agrees that, of these, the relational is by far the more powerful.*

One of the great mistakes we have made over the last two decades is that rapidly evolving educational technologies have been largely *transactional.* Twenty years ago, many very smart people believed that personal computers in classrooms would disrupt education in fundamental ways . . . and they were wrong. Most hardware systems, from desktops to laptops, pads, pods, clickers, smartboards, audio and video recording devices, and vast treasures of software have made it easier and more efficient to push more information at students in a shorter period of time. In the last decade, many more very smart people bet on a new formula for disrupting education, investing hundreds of millions of dollars in the creation and delivery of so-called massively open online courses (MOOCs) that are available for free, many offered by the most prestigious universities on the planet. They believed that MOOCS would bring high-quality learning to millions of people who don't have physical access to teachers and schools . . . and they were wrong. These technologies have opened all kinds of *transactional* access to learning but they largely ignored the critical importance of *relational* learning. Current evidence shows that, for many MOOCs, many learners sign up to take the course, few stick with them, and fewer yet demonstrate significant evidence of learning. As Julie Wilson of Institute for the Future of Learning observed, "How does one engage meaningfully with a discussion thread of over 15,000 'participants'?"

There have been notable exceptions. The growth of the Internet was a pioneering step in relational technology because it allowed individuals in different places to interact in myriad new ways. The explosive adoption of Google Docs in schools and offices around the world took place over a very short period of time, despite resistance from adults who had just become somewhat adept at using the Office suite of software. Applications such as Google Docs enable students and teachers to share and collaborate in real time and with much greater dynamism than in the "old" days of the mid-2000s when we e-mailed documents back and forth. Similarly, the use of gaming in education can create highly collaborative and creative activities that empower students to form relationships based on something other than the fact that they have been assigned to the same classroom. For the most part, however, educational technologies have not been focused on creating richer relationships . . . but I hope that is about to change.

The Stepping Stone: Augmented Reality

We are on the absolute bleeding edge of technology that will completely change the learning equation by providing enhanced *relation-rich* learning outside the traditional school operating system of time, space, and one teacher in the classroom.

Augmented reality (AR) is a stepping stone to virtual reality (VR), and has the potential to completely alter the school operating system. AR, which has crept into schools over the last several years, is a suite of technologies that allows users to superimpose a computer-generated image on their own view of the real world. Students point their smartphone at a math worksheet, click an app, and are linked to a set of support resources on a particular problem. A youngster colors a picture of a dragon, takes a snapshot with another app, and the dragon is dancing in colorful 3D, ready to be copied and pasted into a picture or video of "our" world. A huge company builds manic interest in finding Pokémon cartoon characters hovering virtually in parks and parking lots around the world, and some teachers find a route in this for students to get outside and observe the world outside the classroom.

I visited Bayside STEAM Academy in Imperial Beach, California, where elementary teacher Michael Moran had built an AR sandbox, a simple sandbox connected to a camera, projector, and XBox-type computer. The sandbox enables students to build, move, and change landforms in real time, which are instantly projected down onto the box as colored contours, flowing water, and rain. (It is almost impossible to explain, but if you search "AR sandbox," you can see some short videos that will help you understand in less than a minute.) The elementary students I observed were utterly engaged and elbows deep in sand, fascinated by their collective ability to make land move and change, mimic actual maps, and see how flooding or volcanos or drought might affect their own town. And, in a minute, they could enter a few lines of code and change the settings and parameters all on their own. Augmented models such as this, including 3D holographic simulations, are in their earliest stages of development and promise to re-create what students can do inside and outside the classroom. If used correctly, they will be developed with a pedagogy that encourages or requires relation-rich learning, not isolated work in front of individual LED screens.

The Game Changer: Virtual Reality

But the technology that will most fundamentally change education, that will profoundly change the nature of human connections, that will make the cognitosphere not just a system of knowledge access but rich learning, is virtual reality. We can think of VR as providing two types of revolutionary learning. One is where much of the current work by big companies such as Google, Amazon, and Microsoft is focused. They are providing hardware and software that allow users with a headset to transport to a virtual

But the technology that will most fundamentally change education, that will profoundly change the nature of human connections, that will make the cognitosphere not just a system of knowledge access but rich learning, is virtual reality.

world of their choosing, to wander through an art museum, swim over a coral reef, fly through the Grand Canyon, or explore a complete fantasy land. These are incredibly powerful experiences that blow apart the constraints of a four-walled classroom and turn the idea of a "field trip" on its head. Over the next decade what you can see and where a teacher can take a class of students in VR will be almost unlimited.

The other powerful direction that VR will take us, and which is already here, will be in allowing those groups of "strangers" that Friedman cites, groups of teachers, students, professors, researchers, or grandparents with time on their hands, to meet in virtual worlds to participate in the flow of the cognitosphere, unconstrained by time and space. Building on the decade-old technology of Second Life, anyone with access to the Internet can listen to a lecture; break into smaller working groups; work collaboratively on white boards, bulletin boards, and shared documents; share and watch videos, slide shows, and websites; visit any point in the universe from planets to protons; and share any kind of digital files with each other . . . all in real time without ever leaving his or her desk or couch. We can already collaboratively build a virtual machine, dissect a virtual cadaver, study at a virtual field station, or critique a virtual painting. Students and teachers can meet and work with knowledgeable peers in virtual replications of anywhere in the universe and places that have never existed, whenever their schedules allow. Learners can network with anyone, anywhere in the world as easily as the travelers of the spice routes met in Venice and the pioneers of the information age continue to mash up in Silicon Valley. In short, we are very close to a quantum increase in that "density of connections" that has been such a turbocharger of innovation for centuries. (It is darn hard to describe such a multisensory experience in just words; readers should search on subjects such as "Virbela," "High

Fidelity virtual reality," "Microsoft Hololens," and whatever completely new technology has erupted in the year you are reading this.)

Since 2015 I have explored the potential intersections between VR and deep learning. At that time I partnered with a consortium of Dallas-based schools that are collectively building a forward-leaning center for transformational leadership in education to offer face-to-face and next-generation virtual professional development. We commissioned the design of a user-friendly 3D virtual space where more than 100 people can meet, talk, share files, watch videos, work on websites and group documents, listen to lectures, and attend breakout sessions, all without getting on an airplane to attend a conference somewhere else. By the time you read this, we will have opened a virtual world to educators, a "meeting place of deep, relation-rich connectivity," using technology that teachers and students already have on their own computing devices. Systems such as this will have the capacity to build on the work that Alex Pentland described in *Social Physics:* monitoring, tracking, and providing feedback in real time about how participants in a virtual world interact, perform, and learn. Are students really engaged? Are their eyes wandering, or closed, or focused on the activity? Who is talking the most and who is listening? How is the group working as a team or not? What specific parts of the activity resonate with the learners and which fell flat? We won't have to guess at these factors that affect great learning anymore; we will soon have the data on a dashboard in front of us all of the time.

There is an enormous obstacle, challenge, and opportunity for educators with the rise of VR: to get educational technology right this time! The hardware and software of VR, similar to all previous technologies we have brought into the classroom, will evolve more quickly than we can adapt to the changes, and that curve will continue to accelerate. What *we* have to do is to evolve a *pedagogy* that takes advantage of the unique relation-rich capacities of VR. We have to avoid making the same mistake we made when we thought computers in the classroom or MOOCS would dramatically revolutionize education. If we don't develop a *relational* pedagogy to go along with *relationable* AR and VR technologies, we will miss the boat again. The last

If we don't develop a relational pedagogy to go along with relationable AR and VR technologies, we will miss the boat again.

thing we need is another reason for people to isolate themselves from the real world, face planted firmly in another electronic device.

Flying through the Grand Canyon while sitting in New Jersey is *really* cool but it is not game-changing. The first enormous impact of VR will be to revolutionize professional collaboration for teachers. According to work conducted by the Boston Consulting Group for the Gates Foundation, Americans spend *$18 billion* a year (most of it your tax dollars) on educational professional development, and study after study proves that *almost all* of that mind-boggling pile of money is wasted in terms of improving student performance. We even know *why* all that money is wasted, thanks to deep and authoritative studies by Stanford's Linda Darling-Hammond and colleagues (2009), the Boston Consulting Group (2014), Jane Cogshall writing for the American Policy Center of the American Institutes of Research (2015), and others. These studies show that the vast majority of professional development is infrequent, discontinuous, lacks focus on what teachers care about, and is conducted by outsiders and visitors, not practicing colleagues and peers. In short, we know that poor professional development for our teachers looks pretty much the same as assembly-line learning for our kids and hinders rather than supercharges our progress up the change curve. VR has the capacity to turn this around.

With VR, teachers can join the flow, learning from each other through frequent, inexpensive, VR meet-ups that are available within a teacher's own busy schedule, tailored to individual needs and interests, and built on peer-to-peer connections. Teachers will be able to share what works with each other; to see what deeper learning looks like in each other's classrooms; to coach and mentor each other based on mutual areas of interest, not the one-size-fits-all, top-down dictates of a district supervisor or a publisher's representative. As Walter Issacson says in *The Innovators,* "Sustained innovation could occur when people with a variety of talents were brought together, preferably in close proximity where they could have frequent meetings and serendipitous encounters."

The real tsunami will arrive when teachers can take that experience and turn to their students and say "reach out into the cognitosphere today; find other students, researchers, teachers, and experts who are working on what interests you; meet and share ideas and data with them; and then report back to our class on what you have learned or built together." Each student's learning contributes to the flow in the system, adding to the creation, sharing, and management of knowledge with global groups of interest-based co-learners. This may seem like a *Star Trek* dream, but the fact of the matter is that it will be a daily occurrence at many "schools" within the next decade.

How We Will Press This Lever

The rise of the cognitosphere is a whole new highway of human social connectivity that is going to change how 4 to 6 billion people in the world interact. Education needs an on-ramp onto that highway *now*, not in 10 or 20 years. Educators need to be embedded leaders, not bystanders in the development of this next tsunami of human connectivity.

How shall educators begin to restructure our learning system to align with the nature of the cognitosphere? How can we create structures that amplify flow rather than restricting it? How can we increase connectivity and the power of networks in the everyday work of our schools? How might we begin to use the tools of augmented and virtual reality in ways that stimulate deeper learning and not get trapped into a losing game of buying the latest new gadget? How do we get and stay on a curve that is already rocketing out of our control? As I quoted whitewater kayak champion Anna Levesque at the beginning of the chapter, the only thing to do is to paddle into the rapids. Or, as Eric Teller told Thomas Friedman, "The new kind of stability has to be dynamic stability. There are some ways of being, like riding a bicycle, where you cannot stand still, but once you are moving it is actually easier. It is not our natural state. But humanity has to learn to exist within this state. We are all going to have to learn that bicycle trick."

Using the framework of this chapter, here are some ways education stakeholders can "learn that bicycle trick" in a world where dynamic balancing is increasingly required.

Building Connectivity: Joining the Cognitosphere

- Support teachers in finding and joining informal collaborations with colleagues inside and outside of your school. These can include weekly Twitter chats, regional EdCamps, or group blog reading and writing. If each teacher in a 10-person team finds 5 to 10 new colleagues, and shares those with the team, suddenly you have 50 to 100 new sources of ideas and opportunities.

- Celebrate and reward those who try something new, run a pilot, or connect with a new network of educators. Hold semiannual or annual "teachers teach teachers" events on campus in place of consultant-led professional development days.

- Develop your own ¾-day teacher workshop and open it to teachers from other schools. Share your successes. Don't charge a fee. Ask experts to join the event via video link to give short talks or hold a Q&A session during the day (yes, I do these all the time for free).

- Join a network of forward-leaning schools, such as Big Picture, Deeper Learning, or EdLeader21, or a consortium of thinkers and doers like The Convergence Center and Transcend Education and others. Reward teachers who reach out and work with colleagues at other network schools and bring those lessons back.

- No matter what hat you wear, model ongoing, connected learning for others. Share articles and ideas via Twitter, or start writing a blog and let colleagues know that is where they will find out about your thinking, your work, and your successes.

- Create conditions for your students to become their own powerful "rivers" in the cognitosphere. Publish student papers and movies, rather than just turning them in to the teacher. Create opportunities for students to work with peers at other schools in areas of common interest.

- Suggest *Creativity, Inc.; Thank You for Being Late; Social Physics;* and *#EdJourney* for group reading and discussion, or watch YouTube videos of talks by Alex Pentland and Adrian Bejan on the nature of flow and how it is reflected in social and learning interactions.

Managing the Steep Curve

- We have to reset our horizons and goals. Although short-term indicators such as average performance on standardized tests give us one set of valuable data, those cannot be our only aiming point. Plan for the capacity our society will have 5 to 10 years from now, not what you have today. Start by stripping your school or district goals down to "what does great learning look like for our students?" and commit to dynamic pursuit of that question as external conditions constantly change.

- Shift the discussion to a longer-horizon mind-set: How do we teach students (and adults) to "paddle fast in the rapids." Teaching a growth mind-set must become core to our mission as educators, not something we talk about in theory. Students, teachers, and administrators should be able to discuss and define their own progress in terms of growth mind-set. Executives should be able to demonstrate their own ability to shift from traditional prediction-based models of management that have been the foundation of their own success to comfort with uncertainty and constantly moving horizons.

- Do *not* get locked into one suite of hardware and software as if it were a long-term solution; it never is. Learning must be increasingly "device agnostic." Buy and use tools that are affordable to replace frequently. One example of this: A few years ago most schools were afraid to allow students to "bring your own device" to school. Now BYOD is becoming much more common, even down to primary grades. Don't fight this; don't "dig in your paddle." Adjust learning practices to the reality that students will increasingly own devices that connect to the cognitosphere, and that is good, if uncomfortable and fraught with security challenges you will have to deal with.

- Follow the kids. They are less afraid of the future, they like trying new things, and often they know about evolving technologies before the adults do. Create a venue for students to share and teach what they are learning outside of school with their peers and their teachers.

Embrace Virtual Reality Learning

- Start VR pilots with tools such as Google Cardboard, which is inexpensive, so you don't have too much sunk cost when the next better thing comes along.

- Focus on pedagogy. Start a task force on developing virtual reality pedagogy. Keep track of what generates real learning outcomes with VR and AR pilots, and what is just "cool stuff." Every time a new idea is shared with the team, make sure you are asking, "Does that get us closer to great, relation-rich learning?" Share your findings via social media and at conferences.

- As they become available, join a virtual meet-up with colleagues at other schools or subscribe to a professional learning short course that is offered in VR on your existing computer.
- Challenge yourself, your teachers, and your students to design augmented reality activities that lead to demonstrably deeper learning outcomes. Have teacher and student teams codevelop rubrics for what makes an augmented or VR activity valid as opposed to "just wow."
- Form a citywide or regional collective to share evolving opportunities and best practices in AR and VR, and connect the team with leading developers such as Google, Samsung, Microsoft, High Fidelity, Virbela, and many others. Try to find developers who have a presence in your city or region and who will send representatives to your school to listen and learn from you and your students.

Challenge to the Big Tech Developers

Finally, an audacious challenge targeted at some big, influential stakeholders that can make a huge difference in the long-term trajectory of education is jump-starting the cognitosphere at scale. The lever we need to press is *not* based on a proprietary technology platform; it is based on a *mind-set* that is ready to develop pedagogy and practices for a world in which learning will be unrestricted by classroom walls, the textbook on the shelf, the time of day, or the people who live close to us. Educators need to get in the game *right now,* sitting side-by-side in the driver's seat with technology developers to ensure virtual reality becomes a liberating tool of education, not just a really cool way to play games and travel around with your head planted in a helmet.

I have urged major developers to do the following:

- Make basic VR free and easily available to everyone on the planet with access to the Internet. Similar to Google Docs, which was a foreign invader in schools less than a decade ago and now is used by a majority of teachers and students who have ready access to computers, free VR environments in which teachers and students can virtually gather and learn should be as easy as turning on the computer and clicking a link.

- Create a "dating service" (the key components of which I have already designed but not published yet) for individuals to seamlessly find and virtually meet up with others who share their interests and learning goals. Teachers who have curriculum, syllabi, and video examples of their deeper learning classrooms should be able to easily and quickly find and connect with other teachers who want to see and learn. A student in Iowa interested in groundwater or stem cells or social justice should just as easily be able to connect "in person" with a professor or lab researcher or fellow student in Mumbai who is working on the same thing.

Big developers must help *create the conditions* for educators to get on the curve and lead it in a direction that will best help our students to succeed. If they build easy, accessible, virtual communities for K–12 education, innovation in education will explode. The thousands of tired teachers who still find time to share their successes in weekly Twitter chats, constrained by 140 character bursts, will *flock* to this virtual space. They will sit, talk, and share with each other: What interests or worries you? What is working? What is not? How can I help? *Try this; it worked for me.* The first users, the walkouts, will be teachers, those 20+% of eager early innovation change agents who are begging for change and don't know how. We know it will work because it always has. Give smart, passionate people the chance to share and create, frequently and easily, and lots of little levers turn into really, really big levers that move even the heaviest rock.

Final Thought

Transformational technologies, from the wheel to the printing press, steam energy, the telephone, radio, air travel, television, personal computing, and the Internet, have never been just about changing how we "do" the mechanics of our lives. Truly transformational technologies enable us to *fundamentally reimagine* our relationship to the world around us, and those transformational technologies have become *increasingly inclusive over the march of human history*. Guttenberg did not merely press blocky lead letters onto paper; he democratized the distribution of knowledge. The Wright brothers built a flying machine, but it was pioneering pilots such as Amelia Earhart who turned that machine into a dream catcher. In the 1960s NASA rocketeers built a towering totem to the audacity of engineers and the entire American ethos. Bill Gates did not just write a new computer operating system; he imagined a world where computers might be accessible to every family in every home. The disruption of Steve Jobs was that he saw a world in which computing was an extension of human expression. Real disruption, similar to great learning, is about changing mind-sets, not just mechanics.

> *Real disruption, similar to great learning, is about changing mind-sets, not just mechanics.*

For innovators this moment in time is comparable to that day in 1876 when Alexander Graham Bell connected two people by a wire; the day when John Kennedy audaciously said we were going to the moon; the year when Edwin Catmul, John Lasseter, and George Lucas created a whole new intersection of storytelling and animation; when Jobs, Wozniak, Gates, and others radically imagined that computing power could be brought down from the corporate high rise to the family living room. Over several years of visiting and working with thousands of educators, I am increasingly convinced that by far the best way for us to transform our system of education is to create massively greater access for teachers to "see, feel, and learn" about deeper learning methods. As a society we need educators to help lead the evolution of the cognitosphere, not just wait for it to arrive.

CHAPTER EIGHT

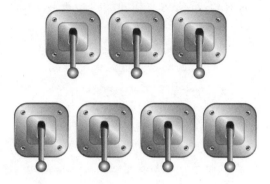

Lever #7
Lead Change from Where You Are

We realized that our purpose was not merely to build a studio that made hit films but to foster a creative culture that would continually ask questions.
Edwin Catmul, cofounder of Pixar Studios

If you don't like something, change it. If you can't change it, change your attitude.
Maya Angelou

From the top of my driveway I can just see the boulder-strewn northern shoulder of Iron Mountain, a half-granite, half-volcanic knob that has become a popular local hike for its steep, rocky, 1,000-foot rise and lordly view across San Diego County, the Pacific Coast, and northern Baja California. On weekends the trail is a traffic jam of hikers, chiseled marathoners in their $150 running shoes, casual tourists wearing flip flops and carrying water in jugs, and courageous senior citizens with twin walking poles and broad-brim hats from REI. The trail is uncomfortably crowded from mid-morning to dark, but one cold, winter weekday, with the sun just rising over the Laguna Mountains to the east, I followed my brother, Brad, up the trail. We made the summit in the full sunlight of one of those Southern California January mornings that most of the Northern Hemisphere only dreams about, a soft Santa Ana breeze blowing east to west keeping the morning *fog at bay and just ruffling the spidery brush of sage and sumac. We could see from the Coronado Islands 10 miles off of Mexico clear around to snowy peaks east of Los Angeles 80 miles away.*

Brad probably thought we would just walk and talk about family stuff; like most brothers, even those who live close by, we don't see each other as much as we should. I had a broader agenda, because Brad is a retired veteran educator—teacher, vice principal, principal, and assistant superintendent, all in large, diverse public schools— and although he and I have discussed, preached, and often argued over the last 40 years about how education can and should change, one thing I know: He changed schools for the better at every stage of his career. So I asked him questions about how he led change in schools where inertia and tradition had held a firm grip for decades, where teachers were vastly more comfortable doing what they had always done and keeping their heads tucked down against the winds of change.

"I always had the best results when I asked myself and others to look out into the future and ask two pretty simple questions," he said. "Ask yourself what you want to think and feel. Change is about head and heart. You won't get change unless you can satisfy both. I ask people to share those and write them down. As a leader, if people know that I am going to support them in reaching those mental and emotional goals, they are going to get there and, as a group, we will all get there as well."

It sounds simple, and in principle it is. The problem is that how to help an organization find and reach what is in their heads and hearts is not something most educators have been trained to do.

In the early 2000s I had the distinct honor and privilege of working with cadets from the United States Military Academy at West Point. In teaching them how to find and solve problems, how to develop and implement creative and strategic goals in ambiguous settings, I learned about the evolving role of "leader" in an organization—the Army—where failures in leadership and decision making can get people killed. In World War II, if an officer said, "fire a shell into that village beyond those trees," the men on the line fired those shells. Now, in conflicts such as Iraq and Afghanistan, where the conditions are less knowable and far more ambiguous, where there are few front lines and where enemies and friends often look very much the same, every private with a rifle has the responsibility to make those life-and-death decisions every day. Now, when an officer says "shoot into that building," it is the right and responsibility of every soldier to make the decision to, in fact, pull the trigger. The Army realizes that fluid environments and rapid change calls for rapid decision-making structures. This is the leading edge of distributed leadership.

Although most decisions made in most schools do not mirror the intensity of those made in a war zone, innovation during times of rapid change requires organizational nimbleness, not rigidity, and that is only possible if we trust and empower people throughout the organization to make decisions: *to lead from where they are*. This chapter is not about the specifics of effective change leadership; there are entire libraries of books and centuries of advice that speak to the nature of great leadership. This chapter is about making at least some of that knowledge available to educators who have been trained in teaching kids to learn but not in leadership, management, and the principles of innovation at a time when these skills are critical to the long-term success of the institution we call "school."

Although there is no single cookbook recipe for changing schools, we do know this: Schools do not change without effective leaders who understand the why, what, and how of change. Cindy Johansen, executive director of Edutopia, the not-for-profit entrusted by George Lucas to align his fortune from making movies with his passion for the future of education, put it simply: "Courageous leadership is really *the* key to organizational innovation. We need to educate upcoming leaders in those skills and what it looks like." In the many schools and districts where I have had the privilege to visit and work, the most obvious, powerful correlation with significant innovation is the ability of those entrusted with leadership to recognize the need to change and then effectively lead the process, regardless of the risks and fears they encounter. What are those skills? What are the key attributes of a courageous leader in a school setting? Although there are many, the four that I have found to be most important in leading change at schools are these:

> *Schools do not change without effective leaders who understand the why, what, and how of change.*

- Modeling risk for others
- Developing effective distributed leadership across the school
- Courage to launch pilots without a guarantee of future success
- Willingness to embrace discomfort and lead others outside their comfort zones

Innovation is far more successful when leadership is distributed throughout an organization, when we don't have to rely on the "top" person to empower change, to give us permission to each take a risk or try something new. In fact, the very premise of this book, what I heard from all of the people whose thinking comprise this book, is that the solutions that will really change schools don't require us to wait on the "top." But in order to build that system and capacity for distributed leadership, we need to train people in how it works. Teachers and school administrators are smart people, but few if any have taken courses in organizational leadership and management, yet those are the skills they need. So let's provide it.

It is one thing to know how to lead an organization in theory and quite another to successfully build an organization that has the actual capacity to change. In schools, so much of that capacity has to do with collective mind-set. As Bo Adams, director of the Mt. Vernon Institute for Innovation, frequently reminds us, "for decades, schools have been focused on *teaching*; we have to refocus on *learning*." In order to make this transition, many things must take place, but in this chapter we focus on creating conditions in which more people across the organization know and feel that they have the empowerment to lead change and the know-how to make it work. Our schools just do not have that empowerment and capacity as part of their cultural DNA right now. A Gallup study in 2014 found that K–12 teachers were the *least* likely among 12 occupational groups studied to agree with the statement, "At work, my opinions seem to count." Perhaps the problem is summed up best in the short, wildly popular allegory on leading change *How Stella Saved the Farm* by Vijay Govindarajan and Chris Trimble, in which we are reminded that "expecting one leader to 'just go make it happen' was a woefully inadequate approach to moving an innovative idea forward."

What Is Missing

We have known for centuries that one of the most powerful drivers of innovative change is the degree of networked connectivity among people inside and outside of the system. Vista Unified School District superintendent Devin Vodicka says that the root of leadership in schools lies with a curious artifact of the system. Over time, says Devin, the education system has evolved to see "all the components as inanimate objects. Transformation is about seeing the pieces as part of a living system, with choices to make and free will and different points of view. When we do this, lots of things become possible. The most important of these is the ability to develop social capital. Connecting people and allowing the development of personal relationships creates space and opportunity for things to ignite within the system that we never even thought possible. The ability to build both internal and external connections has to be at the very top of the list for effective educational leadership" in schools, says Devin.

Unfortunately, K–12 education frequently fails those on whom we rely as leaders when it comes to developing skills such as how to acquire and build social capital. Before becoming a public school principal, Steve Baca learned a few things about leadership as a cadet and quarterback of the football team at West Point (which is just a coincidence relative to my earlier citation of work with West Point) and later as an Army officer. He left the Army to return to his hometown of Santa Fe, New Mexico, where high-performing schools on the clean, wealthy, tourist-rich east side of the city are separated by just a few miles from poorly performing schools on the poor, dusty west side of town with its working-class neighborhoods, trailer parks, and narrow strip malls. When Steve came home, he went to work on the western side of town, trying to turn around some of the state's poorest performing schools.

"If there is one thing we learn in the Army that applies to schools," says Steve, "it's that there are no bad units, only bad commanders. The number one lever of organizational change is the leader, and in order to be effective, leaders have to have control to put the power where it needs to be: with teachers, students, parents, wherever. Lacking that power and the knowledge of how to use it, not to do everything from the top-down, but to give real power to those who need it, organizations will not change." Steve agrees that the K–12 education system has a terrible track record at developing leaders. "We [education] have done leadership professional development as a 'drive-by,'" says Steve, "and just hope that those we task with leading somehow know what to do. They don't."

Steve says there are two specifics that are needed in educational leadership training. The first is that programs, institutions, and graduate schools that certify leaders have to change their approach from "spend *x* hours in course work" to "at least a 50–50 model," in which at least half of the time is spent in practical work and internships.

Schools have to shift away from a top-down leadership model to a more distributed model, and we have to train leaders in how to make that leadership model work.

New school leaders, says Steve, are largely swinging in the dark when they are placed in positions that require leadership skills. "Most came from the classroom and want to be site leaders because the pay is better and they default back to 'this is how I ran my classroom,' because that is what they know and the experience they have." Second, says Steve, schools have to shift away from a top-down leadership model to a more distributed model, and we have to train leaders in how to make that leadership model work. "Right now," says Steve, "too many principals and district officer leaders are stuck in the mode where their first response is 'do what you are told, and if you don't know how I will send you to a one-hour professional development course.'"

Because many school leaders lack the basic skills of effective leadership, we are stuck constantly reinventing the wheel, even though we know what does and does not work. Steve says that in his experience "we waste incredible amounts of money just trying stuff and then abandoning it. Successful businesses have it right. People in successful organizations are allowed to make mistakes and learn from those. We know that where we bring that mind-set and those processes into schools, both adults and students learn better, but that mind-set has not percolated either as fast or as deeply as it needs to in our education system."

Sharing the Leadership Experience

In my view, few school leaders have been as successful at leading an organization to develop massive capacity for thoughtful learning and innovative change as Chris Lehmann, founding principal of Philadelphia's Science Leadership Academy (SLA). Chris says that what makes SLA so successful as an exemplar of school organizations is "understanding what mission work looks like, and developing a school organization consistent with that mission such that we don't pivot every time something new comes along.

We have the skills to stay true to that mission and get better at it over time, regardless of the tugs and pulls of interest groups." Chris's book *Building School 2.0,* coauthored with teacher Zac Chase, is a must-read, the kind of book one can open to any page and find, within its simple, clear examples, great new footholds on leading change that any educator can implement tomorrow in the classroom, office, or the school hallways.

Although SLA is an exemplar of deeper learning, the real passion of their team is to create the conditions that enable *others* to replicate their success at scale. Around the country, in the last five years, there has been an explosion of formal and informal mini-conferences, workshops, EdCamps, and meet-ups among like-minded educators who are short on budgets, long on energy and expertise, and don't wait for a directive from the district office to share what they know. This is the kind of fertile ground that the SLA team loves to nurture. Larissa Pahomov of SLA says that similar to many other districts, the School District of Philadelphia has four or five professional development days each year. "Several years ago Central High School started offering a teacher-led, teacher-driven day where educators throughout the district submitted proposals for workshops. We took that model and combined it with our annual EduCon in January" and in 2016 SLA ran a first-of-its kind conference for all-comers in the Philadelphia area. "The focus of our conference was really on the nuts and bolts of how we make our learning style work in a large, urban, public school setting." Half of the presenters were from SLA and the rest from other schools, and because all are school employees the event was free for all of the more than 225 attendees from dozens of local schools . . . as well as the 10 visitors from the mayor's office of job, career, and counseling programs.

"A lot of teachers are not conditioned to think they have something worth presenting," says Larissa, "when in fact they are the most knowledgeable about what is working and what is not. I talked to one colleague who is really an outstanding teacher and her response to me was 'I don't know what I have that is worth sharing,' but that is because in the past, professional training was something that was done 'to' teachers. They are never given the opportunity to share, when that should be the norm, because that is how they become good at leading change in their own schools." Larissa said that within a couple of weeks of the conference she had received e-mails from people at other schools with the same theme: "Why aren't *we* doing that? That's not tough; we just had never thought of it."

Formal Training in Leadership

The skills of change leadership, although evolving in the 21st century, are not a mystery; they are taught in every good business school and management training program. What has been missing is access to that training for the vast majority of educators, placed in the context of schools. And though many theories and successful practices hold true for all organizations, schools are, in fact, special places that do not act or operate like a bank, a manufacturer, or a high-tech company. If we are going to promote innovation in education, which relies on a distribution of leadership across the school, rather than reserving the role of "leader" for the principal or the superintendent, then we have to provide this training and professional growth across a much broader set of teachers as well.

In my own practice, as I focus first with schools and districts on setting a forward-leaning vision that aligns their resources to their greatest aspirations, there always comes a time when we have to put theory to practice, to engage in the often messy work of making change a reality. I have increasingly partnered with Julie Wilson of the Institute for the Future of Learning, whose wheelhouse is "the human side of school change." She has built on more than 15 years at Harvard teaching individuals and organizations about the art and science of change with the nuance of schools and is remarkably effective at helping not just senior administrators but also classroom teachers see how they, too, can be a nucleating force for innovative change. I know that a school team will succeed in their work when I see teachers, many of whom have never had a single course or lesson in how to lead a collaboration of colleagues, quickly apply the simple tools that Julie gives them, such as finding group strengths, organizing effective meeting time, setting group norms for sustainable collaboration, and getting others to share a common vision.

The role of leadership at all levels of education, what I call "leading from where you are," is finally beginning to take a marquee spot among traditional and new types of professional education organizations. The University of Virginia's Darden School of Business and the Curry School of Education have created a "Partnership for Leaders in Education" program that trains educators in the fundamentals of successful turnarounds, removing barriers to organizational redesign, creating cultures of high expectation and effective collaboration, the use of data in decision making and mid-course corrections, and action and communication planning. A consortium of Dallas-based schools has partnered with the Simmons School for Education and Human Development at Southern Methodist University to create the Center for Transformational Leadership, which will develop and offer a unique portfolio of PK–12–focused professional growth programs that are based on how teachers and administrators can develop their skills as effective educational leaders, particularly in a time of rapid change. And at the University of Pennsylvania, the School Leadership Program borrows from business school models for their executive format that allows participants to dive deeply into leadership training without interrupting their careers and requires a 240-hour mentored internship to build on the power of practice over classroom learning.

The role of leadership at all levels of education, what I call "leading from where you are," is finally beginning to take a marquee spot among traditional and new types of professional education organizations.

In her long career in K–12 education, ex-superintendent Carmen Coleman believes that we have now passed the point where a shift to a model of deeper learning is even a question; it has become the imperative that requires this kind of fundamental training in change leadership. "Over the last decade," says Carmen, "I started to see that there were schools where the kids looked a lot like ours, no more or less smart, but doing the most amazing things because they were deeply engaged in their learning. Even the kids know it; I have had 6th and 7th graders tell me how simple it is: 'we learn better if we care about it and enjoy what we are doing.' I realized that 'we' [leaders and teachers] were just getting in the way and we didn't know it because we did not know any better."

Recognizing this key need to spread the fundamentals of how schools change across a much broader universe of educators, in 2010 Carmen helped found the Next Gen Leadership Academy, an extension of the University of Kentucky School of Education that brings school teams together six or seven times in a year to think about the most essential learning outcomes, the experiences needed to generate those outcomes, and how those experiences differ from what takes place in most schools today. They bring in teachers and administrators from schools with effective leadership talent so teachers can talk to peers, and not just trainers. Then, says Carmen, teams just "pick a place to start and start the transformation. Our guiding question is how to help teachers and administrators and future teachers and administrators see the possibilities and think bigger than we are right now. We have to keep our eyes on what is happening locally and regionally, but it's even more important to know what is happening all over the world, sometimes in schools that look very different from our own. We find educators really *want* this; they get it if they just see it. Most teachers really *want* kids to be excited about their learning; we just lost sight of that."

Carmen says that developing the educator-leader is the goal, but it is a chicken-and-egg problem: There has to be multilevel agreement to build a culture that *allows* and *expects* real change leadership to effectively evolve. They quickly realized that they needed to get out of the university setting and engage with teachers on their own turf. "We packed up some of the faculty of the school of education and came out to listen and stay connected and ask 'what can we do for you?'" says Carmen. Once they have interest within a district to provide this kind of leadership and classroom training, they are equally careful to get permission and buy-in from the district and site levels. The result has been that they are seeing real transformation starting to bud, first in thinking and conversation, and then in practice, all during a time when, according to Carmen, "nothing much has changed at the state level. The big question we as educators need to ask as we try to change such a stubbornly stuck system is 'do you want to see incremental improvement or do you want a real game changer?' We can't wait for permission. It reminds us all of the Henry Ford quote: 'If I had asked people what they wanted, they would have said faster horses.'"

Scaling Up

I found another powerful example of scaled-up leadership training that started as a service for Wisconsin public schools but has percolated much more broadly in recent years. More than 40 years ago, the Wisconsin state legislature created 12 Cooperative Educational Service Agencies (CESAs) to provide educational services in partnership with schools and districts. In 2009 a group of Wisconsin educators in CESA 1, which hugs the southeast corner of the state, asked how they could make fundamental changes in their schools that were *not* mandated by the state or federal governments but *were* developed, understood, and embraced by teachers. They were frustrated that they kept spending more and more money on traditional-style professional development, but nothing much was changing in many classrooms. They realized that the solutions were not going to come from the capital but by empowering change leaders at a much more local level. Jim Rickenbaugh, the director for the Institute for Personalized Learning within CESA 1, says that when they started, they thought changing learning was about changing how teachers teach. "But that does not move the needle unless we change the role of the learner," says Jim. "Learning is what we need to focus on; instruction is how we support learning. And we found that we do that best by moving from a 'mandate approach' to an 'interest approach,' from a compliance domain to a commitment domain. We want to dramatically change learning for the students to be more personalized, and if we can give our teachers an experience and understanding of what personalized learning is, they are then able to do that *with*, not *for*, their students."

> *If we can give our teachers an experience and understanding of what personalized learning is, they are then able to do that* with, not for, *their students*

Similar to most states, Wisconsin did not have a pot of money sitting around to develop and test a new approach to learning, so CESA 1 designed a program that only used the money that was already available to schools and "would not come and go, like outside grants. And," says Jim, "we don't want schools to have to add layers of staff. They may move some people around, but they need to be able to create and lead real systemic change without adding new staff and more expense." Individual schools reassign resources: existing funds for professional development, Title 1 money, or just by making changes to how they operate, such as the school that found out it had playground supervisors they really did not need. "The tipping point comes when schools and districts move from examples in a hallway or a building to 'this is how we do business,'" says Jim. "This takes time, but we are seeing movement in some districts from just general discussion to real, long-term sustainable action."

Jim and the others who lead the CESA 1 institute see themselves as a network of practitioners, not a product or set of precooked services. "We are not limited by politics," says Jim. "We grow and respond with our member districts and schools." As of 2016 they were serving and connecting with 48 different school districts, only about half of which were in their own region in Wisconsin. The other half were scattered throughout the remainder of the state, as well as in Minnesota, Nebraska, Missouri, Illinois, and Texas. "The obstacles to replicating this kind of work are more perceived than real," says Jim. "Teacher licensing is based on instruction, not learning, and that has to change. Mostly it is just fear of something we have not done in the past. When we change that mind-set, most educators realize this is what they really want to be doing."

How We Will Press This Lever

We have to stop treating schools as something separate from the other great institutions of our society, walled off from the knowledge and history of dynamic, creative invention that have been the signature hallmark of human civilization for the last 600 years. The great transformation that is inevitable in education in the next decade or two will be the shift from stasis to dynamism, from teaching most of the same things in mostly the same ways to learning and working within the vastly more fluid flow of the cognitosphere.

This transformation requires an added set of skills for those who fuel this powerful engine: the adults with whom we entrust our children. They are often among the brightest, most dedicated, most selfless people in our society, and they deserve every tool and resource we can provide. It is not enough for educators of the future to know their subject; they also have to know how to lead, how to lead change, and how to help their school organization create and build sustainable success when the ground is less predictable and stable than it has been in the past.

Getting Started for K–12 Educators

Those higher in the school hierarchy need to show others that they are willing to move outside of their own comfort zones; they must model innovation for others to follow. Try a new technology. Empower others to make decisions, and support them in those decisions. Support a pilot program even though you don't have the longitudinal study to prove that it is superior to what is being taught today. Be vulnerable, and let others see that vulnerability; let others know you don't have all of the answers and create structures at the school that allow and require others to find those answers for themselves. Publicly celebrate appropriate risk-taking by students and teachers as they demonstrate their willingness to go outside of their own comfort zones.

- Add books such as *Building School 2.0* by Lehmann and Chase and *Creating Cultures of Thinking* by Ron Ritchhart to faculty summer reading options, and use these to focus faculty discussions over the year: How might we embed the skills in these books into the daily practice at our school? Ask teacher cohorts to pick two to three skills in these books that resonate with them, put them into practice, and share the results at faculty meetings and short internal EdCamps.
- Find or start a faculty leadership "boot camp" for your teachers. Adopt a school or district policy of "teachers teaching teachers" in which you send a few teachers to advanced professional learning in the areas of leadership skills, and then those "leaders" come back and pass their learning forward during regular professional development days or in a summer institute format.

Taking It to the Next Level

- Find one of the college or business school programs that is already tailored to educational leadership, and send a few teachers each year. Make these spots available to classroom teachers who are *not* department or grade-level chairs but who show a willingness to adopt new thinking about how your school operates. Incentivize early adopters in your school who are willing to learn and share these skills; sometimes just public recognition is enough reward to motivate people to do what they want to do in the first place.

- Find and bring in skill-building consultants who can help construct a system of distributed leadership in your schools. These consultants give traditional teachers the tools they need to take risks and make decisions on their own. Most important, these consultants should build capacity in your own teachers to teach others, with the goal of *not* needing outside consultants after the first few years.

- Business schools need to know that there is a demand for this kind of course; give them that demand. Reach out to other schools and districts and collectively contact a local or regional college-level business school. Partner with them to create or expand a program focused on educator leadership. Cocreate a curriculum with their faculty members and provide them an initial stream of teacher students for the program. Build in a certification for the course work that participants can add to their résumé.

The Role of College and Business Schools

- In turn, college and university graduate schools of business should supply the K–12 market with courses and programs of organizational management, organizational leadership, and change leadership *specifically* tailored for educators. This will require faculty at the business schools to empathetically understand the unique challenges faced by education and design a program to meet those challenges. These programs need to address the varying needs of everyone in the K–12 system, from classroom teacher to superintendent.

- These programs need to be highly accessible to our hard-working, underpaid educator corps. It is easy to create an expensive three-week summer management course for superintendents; we already have those. We need our talented business schools to add programs that are affordable and that are offered at times and in ways that are accessible to rank-and-file teachers and administrators.

- This may *never* be a profit maker for the business schools, the best of which today are staffed with faculty members who consult with powerful companies for large, well-deserved fees. Our business school faculties need to see this partnership with our K–12 schools as something that is valued and greatly needed for the future of our society; it is quasi–pro bono work that needs to take root if we want our K–12 schools to change at scale.

Schools are *not* like other businesses, but there are an increasing number of overlapping points of interest. Right now, businesses schools are our best repository of the art and science of change management and leadership, and we have to open that rich vein to many, many more of our educators. We have started to see this, as a few universities build bridges between schools of business and education, as a few K–12 schools send their administrators to get an MBA or to take course work dedicated to modern leadership practice, and as consultants build their libraries of management-focused professional development.

But the pace is way too slow and the spread of this training is way too uneven. If we don't train our teachers and administrators in the skills of leadership and change management, the schools won't change and it will be our own fault; we will have confused a bold plan for change with the hope that it will just happen, and we know better. We have the knowledge, the resources, and the creativity; we just need the will. Like other challenges in this book, some leaders in the business schools and the K–12 systems will say, "We can't do that because . . .," and they will fill in the blank with valid reasons. It has always been so. Others, I hope, will gather the incredible talent and resources over which they have moral or titular control . . . and just do it.

CHAPTER NINE

How *You* Will Transform Education

*You see things and you say, "Why?" But I dream things that never were and
I say, "Why not?"*

George Bernard Shaw, borrowed and tweaked
by Bobby Kennedy and others

*We know that dramatic change is possible in our K–12 system of education. We see the
campfires of innovation and the positive results all around us. We see the real changes in
the real lives of real kids. Now the question is, do we have the collective will and imagination to bring these changes to scale, perhaps not to 100% of schools and students in the
next 10 to 15 years but to a significant majority? Do we have the courage to prepare this
generation of students for the world that lies ahead of them, or will most of us kick that
can down the road and hope that someone else does it in the future or that the problem
will somehow just go away? Will we continue to point fingers at "the others" and say that
solving the problem is* their *responsibility because of a job title or because a small group
of self-interested voters showed up to the polls last year or because the problem is complex and hard to solve? Will we continue to fight contrarian battles against vested interest
groups and thereby cede them the power to keep things as they are? Or will we look at
our own kids and those of our neighbors and realize what is right in front of us, that it is
our* responsibility, *that we can change this most critical of social institutions by pressing
the levers that are available to us?*

I argued in *#EdJourney* that this evolving next generation of education has vastly more affinity to a natural ecosystem than a socially engineered system. The levers I have proposed in this book, based on the input from so many knowledgeable experts around the country, will help that system evolve thoughtfully and not chaotically. Many of these levers are already in motion, and there are many ways for individuals and schools to get started without a major commitment to dramatic change. This new education system will not be handed to us by some working group or presidential commission sitting around a table or conducting community workshops. The process won't be centrally controlled by large entities such as the Department of Education or a small group of powerful individuals, corporations, or not-for-profit organizations. It is evolving out of a widely distributed and (this is critical) *symbiotically connected* system of people, schools, businesses, researchers, and funders and through shared trials, failures, and courageous retrials. The process will be accelerated by greater connectivity among the enormous tide of stakeholders who share a critical stake in the future of education . . . our kids.

> *This new education system will not be handed to us by some working group or presidential commission sitting around a table or conducting community workshops.*

In the afterglow of evolution and revolution, the winners write the story. But the reality is that with all types of change, even those for which there are only great intentions, there are winners and losers. In most social revolutions, people die. In any process of natural evolution some species survive and others do not. Even within those species that adapt and survive, individuals that do not receive the mutated genes that lie at the root of biological evolution don't survive with the same statistical abundance as others. That's the thing about evolution and revolution: Success is not determined by any single individual but by the cumulative impacts of communities, species, nations, social groups, organizations, and businesses that are much larger than the single individual. That's a tough lesson for schools where we rightly try to value each individual, but it is an inevitable measure of change. To some extent we each have to ask a difficult question: Will I, or my colleagues, or my students, or my school survive and thrive? How can I make sure?

It will be easy to see some of the suggested ways to press the levers at the end of each chapter in this book as pipe dreams, doomed to failure because the obstacle of inertia is too great for anyone to overcome, and that is absolutely true: *We* have to overcome them together. So in this penultimate chapter I suggest some additional very specific ways that stakeholder groups can make a real difference, right now, without a large bankroll or a new set of laws.

Don't try to do everything: Just pick one and start rolling.

Teachers

No group can and will influence the future of education more than our teachers. Teachers are the engine of powerful, relation-rich learning. With that great power comes the greatest responsibility. Although teachers are constrained to varying degrees by resources, standards, traditions, and sometimes bosses that we hope will lead but who do not, many of them can change the learning system piece by piece in ways that will cumulatively have dramatic impact, first on their own students and then on the entire system. I know the obstacles that teachers face, and I know that sometimes their best intentions are frustrated. But I also know that it is often the teachers who say, "We are going to charge ahead," who take authority where it is available, who gather with others of like mind and passion . . . and suddenly they find that they are leading from the front, with others begging to follow.

Teachers, along with your students, you are positioned at the center of learning. You can press on every one of the big levers in this book. We can't charge ahead if we don't have some clear idea of where we want to go, so your first mission is to *learn* through the eyes and experience of a professional educator.

- Learn how to create a deeper learning experience from your colleagues in the next classroom, down the hall, in the next building, at the next campus, and in schools around the region, country, and world. Research deeper learning via websites such as Edutopia and the Deeper Learning Network and many others.

- Learn about student assessment strategies and options that measure what we value, and steal the templates for those from schools that already have a track record of success. Suggest, and if need be demand, that your school research and join with others who are developing new measures and reporting of student performance that balance academic and noncognitive growth.
- Reach out to colleagues in your city or region; find out how they and their schools are partnered with business and nonprofits in the community and bring those stories back to your school. Join a Twitter chat once a week, create a blog reading list with a few teaching friends, or launch an EdCamp once every six months in your town.
- Find out "the possible" in schools that are like yours and schools that are very much *not* like yours. Remember that innovation comes by seeking out others at the margins of our mutual experience; don't be afraid to reach out, because there are a few million of you and, together, you know pretty much all we need to know!

With your learning, you need to commit to *grow,* as individuals and as the powerful collective that you are. The greatest pressure you can exert on the levers of change is to commit to change schools from places of *teaching* to places of *learning.* This is the key to shifting from a school that acts like an assembly line to one where you and your students have created a learning path together.

- Let go of the mental anchor that says you must already be expert in the classroom. Embrace the freedom that comes with saying to your students "I don't know exactly how this is going to turn out, but we will get there together."
- During faculty meetings and meetings with your administrators next year, ask questions such as "What does great learning look like to us?" and "How might we dramatically boost student engagement?" Gather answers on sticky notes in just a few minutes. Then start the discussion about how you can set aside all of the stuff you do at your school that is *not* on that path and focus on what is.
- For your ongoing professional development and graduate degrees, attend postsecondary schools of education that offer significant training in deeper learning practices that have a program that

prepares you for the future of education, not just the past and the present. Demand that professional training from outside consultants aligns with what you and your colleagues value, what will make you a better teacher in a deeper learning environment, not a cookbook recipe that has been developed for mass consumption by the "average" teacher.

Finally, *act*. The rock of education is stuck largely because people refuse to act in the face of their own fears and the obstacles that have grown up around us. Some of those fears and obstacles are real, and some are not; they are convenient excuses we all use to avoid that which is uncomfortable.

- View yourself as a leader; embrace the discomfort of making a change in your practice this year. Pick one of these levers, perhaps in cooperation with a group of like-minded colleagues, and just start "doing." Link up via social media and your many professional organizations with others who are pressing the same lever and share your successes and failures.
- Share your thinking and evidence of what you are doing differently in the classroom and why with your parents via social media and every time they visit the school. Tell them that if they like what they see to lobby the principal, superintendent, and school board for more of the same.
- Volunteer to help design and lead a pilot program that brings students and community resources together in a student-centered, growth-oriented, long-term learning partnership. Be the education resource for the partnership; ensure that these community-school partnerships evolve with a laser focus on the long-term best interests of the students.
- With your site, grade level, or subject cohort, or in your professional learning community, set a target to phase out hard-copy textbooks to the extent allowable by your laws and regulations.

Finally, act. *The rock of education is stuck largely because people refuse to act in the face of their own fears and the obstacles that have grown up around us.*

Lobby alongside your parents that cost savings from those textbooks be redirected to professional growth funds.

I can't fail to note that teachers have one more way to press the levers of change. All too frequently I am asked by a passionate, visionary, hardworking, but frustrated teacher, "What do I do if my school just does not want to change? What if my principal or superintendent or the school board is not supporting what I know is a better way of learning?" Sometimes the answer is, "You have to leave." None of us can solve the problem by ourselves, and if the obstacles in your way are truly too great, then you have to make a decision: Do I stay and contribute to the inertia, or do I find another school or another leader where they are pressing the levers with me, not against me? Some teachers, like some families, have these options, and others do not. If there is another school in the district, or the district next door that sounds like some of those in this book, watch for openings, even if that first job is perhaps not the perfect one. Great teachers rise to the top, particularly in systems that value creativity and risk-taking. Your greatest contribution to the changes we need in education just might be getting on a team that really does want to lean on these levers.

School Site and District Administrators

If teachers are the group that can collectively make the most difference to each student, site and district administrators are the group that can, if they press hard, change schools *at scale*. There is good news and bad in that statement: You are the group that most often represents the biggest forces of inertia, and you also have the most leverage to overcome that inertia. Here are some of the tangible steps you can take, right now, to provide real weight to these levers of change:

- In addition to learning alongside your teachers, you have the ability to bring together vast arrays of resources on which your teachers need to draw. Harness the incredible power of connected collaboration. Get together with decision-making colleagues from surrounding districts, make a formal commitment to each other, and take the lead on the challenge to create deeper learning exemplar schools in your areas. Pull out a map and figure out where to start transforming schools to a deeper learning system to make these exemplars most accessible to most of your other teachers and families.

- Invite parents from across the district to see what deeper learning looks like. Rather than fearfully shying away from marketing the exemplar schools because it might pull students away from your more traditional schools, embrace them as levers to *change* those other schools *before* your families abandon them.

- Next year, gather with your district-level colleagues in the city or region to create an agenda for much deeper partnerships with your regional graduate schools of education and business. Host imagination and design collaborations with deans and faculty members; make sure to invite business, nonprofit, and city and state leaders or representatives to attend. Create an action-oriented agenda focused on providing teachers with affordable, accessible training in post–industrial age learning and organizational leadership models.

- Next year, call an initial "imagination and design" meeting of local businesses, higher education, and nonprofit leaders to share national best practices in school community partnerships. Set real goals to establish those partnership programs. Reach out to some of the cities and organizations where these already exist and steal their templates for success.

- Set a goal of offering balanced student assessments and transcripts that measure student progress in what you actually value: a combination of academic and noncognitive growth and understanding.

- Reach out to local employers and business leaders to help outfit and maintain a virtual reality learning lab in your schools. Showcase teachers who are using augmented and virtual reality as learning connections and research tools.

- Change purchasing policies to take advantage of open educational resources (OER). Start next year with stakeholder input and feedback. Set targets to phase out the use of mass publication texts. When needed, lobby regional, county, or state regulators to streamline purchasing of OER and adopt policies to ensure that OER curriculum and materials support mandated standards and learning objectives. Redirect savings to faculty professional development budgets.

- Next year, launch a long-term education program for middle and high school parents and students that looks at the evolving trends in college admissions and begins to dispel the mythology that only a small number of colleges offer "the best" opportunities for our students.

Parents

In the past, parents have been limited in how they can interact with and influence schools. Some of those pathways are hugely valuable to schools: volunteering in the classroom, supporting teachers, or taking on helpful governance roles. Other pathways are destructive, when parents seek to lever their own self-interests over the long-term interests of students. In this evolving ecosystem of radically greater choice, parents will become the single largest influence group in shaping the demand curve for education that meets their different needs.

Parents, here are some specific ways you can start to influence change right now:

Learn how education is changing and what options are offered in your community.

- Look across your local district and see if there is a school that is breaking the traditional mold. Learn about schools in your community that offer deep, rich partnership opportunities with companies, nonprofit organizations, or local colleges and universities. If you find one, go and visit with your child and see if moving to a school of deeper learning is what aligns most closely to your hopes and aspirations for that child.
- Educate yourself about the myths and realities of college admissions, what colleges value, and which colleges or postsecondary education or job-preparation programs might be best for your child. Learn about colleges that value who your child really is and what he or she aspires to be, more than how well he or she performed on a test in high school. Dig past the meaningless college rating systems; there are hundreds of great colleges and universities in America and overseas, and you can shop for the one that is right for *your* child, not right for the *Princeton Review*.

Ask, lobby, and, if needed, *demand* that your schools and district have the courage to break out of the past. I encourage parents to be heard, as consumers, users, and funders of education . . . in appropriate ways! It does little good to bring anger and accusation into the room; bring knowledge, examples, data, and stories. Most professional educators share a deep passion for what is best for our children, and they need your *help* pressing these levers, not your directives.

- Meet with your principal or head of school, or go to a school board meeting and ask, "How might we be the school that leads?" First suggest, and then demand, that high schools offer student assessments and progress reports that measure what school leaders claim are the most important outcomes of a K–12 education, and help your school to find ways to communicate that to college admissions offices.
- Lobby school boards and teachers to take advantage of modern, updatable, digital, *free* curriculum and materials and to redirect wasted textbook budgets toward much-need professional development and collaboration time for teachers to retool their teaching practices. Scream loudly (but politely) that your tax or tuition dollars are being literally thrown down the trash chute of mass publication textbooks. Share authoritative public research on this waste with your school board and district office, and with the local newspapers and news channels.

Finally, *choose;* exercise your right of choice in what is now an open education marketplace.

- The single largest lever that will transform education in the next 20 years is the movement of families from schools that are not meeting their needs to ones that are. If you have a choice of where to send your child to school, vote with your feet and move to those schools. For the sake of your kids, make these choices carefully and infrequently; the last thing children need is to jump around schools every few years or to have mom and dad obsess over every little imperfection they see in their current school.
- Young kids don't have to start preparing for college in elementary school, so resist the urge to try to quantify everything at your school

in terms of rankings. Ask your school leaders how they are teaching and measuring student growth in noncognitive skills and habits such as mindfulness and personal wellness.

Unfortunately, not all families have the same options to choose; they are trapped by poverty, special needs, geography, or limited options where they live. In this case I wish evolution were smoother and more equitable, but it is not. Over time, I believe, the models of great learning will percolate to more, not fewer, communities, and more, not fewer, families will have these options open to them.

Students

Students have been the outsiders of school design, which is of course absurd because they are at the center of what we do. Schools and districts allow the token student member on the board, convene student leadership councils to offer advice on topics that are distant tangents to the core principals of learning, and politely ignore any real interactions with students on a strategic level. In most schools, students don't have a real voice, which is why I suggest students press levers that work despite this system, not necessarily because of it.

- If you love what you are doing at your school, tell your parents and teachers.
- If you really *don't* love what you are doing at your school, tell your parents and teachers (respectfully and thoughtfully).
- Ask your parents if there are other schools in your area where students get to take a big role in their own learning, and go visit those schools.
- Educate yourselves about which colleges value and offer what you are interested in and which value you, not just your test scores, during the admissions process.
- Sign up for elective courses that interest you, not just those that might look good on a college application.
- Politely but firmly demand that your teachers and administrators include student voices in setting assessment strategies so

you know what is expected in a course and why. Ask to work *with* your teachers in defining measures of success in each course; many will look at you as if you are a bit crazy, but some will invite you into the process, and those are the teachers to get to know better!

- Educate your parents and teachers about new and evolving websites that, like Khan Academy and Wolfram Alpha, help you learn in new ways. Often you find out about these long before the adults do! Suggest ways that these can be brought into the learning system that help you understand your work and reduce stress for you and your teachers.

Business and Community Leaders

If there is a single point of radical departure that will mark the change from the schools of the past to those we need, it is the dissolution of the hard boundary between "school" and world. This will create enormous opportunities for leaders and organizations throughout the community – businesses, nonprofits, clubs, and individuals—to help bring about much-needed transformation. Our children are a *community* resource; education is a *community* function; schools are a *community* responsibility. Forward-looking community leaders see the inherent link between how we prepare our students for the future and how well our communities will respond to the challenges that the future holds. Your role is not to tell the professional educators what to do but to work with them, offering your talent, time, and treasure in ways that are unique to you and your experiences.

Researchers at the Harvard Business School and the Boston Consulting Group, in partnership with the Bill and Melinda Gates Foundation, surveyed thousands of superintendents from across the country in 2013 to find out how businesses *are* supporting education and how they *want* businesses to support their schools (Rivkin et al., 2013). The findings were clear: The vast majority of business support for schools is what the report terms "checkbook philanthropy," which generally supports short-term goals or individual students in the form of money, scholarships, or donation of goods. Although this help is certainly welcome, the superintendents wanted businesses "to help them understand, and develop in their students, the skills that will allow students to succeed in the workforce" through deeper and long-lasting relationships such as internships for students, work on education policy, and transference of expertise in organizational leadership and change management.

Here is a list of actions that you, as a leader in your community, can take in the coming year to build an on-ramp to this future for your local and regional schools:

- Take a proactive role in learning about the different schools in your area, and support those that are willing to take risks, engage their students, and try to break the traditional mold of learning. Call your district superintendent or the principal at your child's school. Offer to host, facilitate, or support exploratory meetings on deep, rich community school partnerships. Task one person in your company to take responsibility for developing capacity at your company for active, student-centric partnerships with your K–12 schools. Set up partnerships and internships with schools and loudly publicize the benefits you see for your organization and for the students. Drive demand through what you know well: the marketplace.

- Create a detailed strategy that enables your employees to interact directly with students and teachers in local K–12 schools. Make local K–12 education one of your top two priorities for company-directed philanthropic support, particularly via volunteerism. If they bring a talent that the teachers and students need, people do more to change schools than even money.

- Provide leadership training seminars for teachers and administrators from your local district. If you do not have the in-house expertise for this, partner with a local or regional college, provide or share the costs, and host the program at your business.

- Help superintendents and principals learn how to scale innovation. Businesses are often successful because they have run pilot programs and understand how to scale these pilots up to "production" levels. School systems need this expertise as we move from relatively isolated but highly successful pilots such as those we have seen in this book, to district-wide adoption.

- Provide a small amount of matching funds to double the power of grants awarded by foundations in support of building a set of open educational resources at your local school. Join the parents in lobbying for smart use of *your* tax dollars!

Philanthropists and Foundations

When one group is stuck, it is often up to another to step in, and this is the critical role that outside funders play in education. Innovation in the private sector relies on venture capitalists who risk investment in hopes of future rewards. In the nonprofit sector, philanthropists and foundations are the sources of venture capital, the fuel for designing and testing solutions that fall outside the bounds of traditions and norms. This support promotes courage, nimbleness, creativity, and thinking beyond the obstacles of inertia.

We see today some enormous commitments on the part of outside funding sources, and if they focus on potentially game-changing levers such as those I have described in this book, we will dramatically accelerate the evolution and equity of education change. Specifically, foundations can *help create the conditions in which innovation thrives*. It is crystal clear that we are rapidly getting to the point where we know *what* to do; the conditions that move that knowledge from isolated examples to a much larger scale is where foundation venture capital needs to focus.

- We need greater *density* of school examples, so teachers, administrators, and parents can see what is possible, what aligns with their own vision of great learning. I urge the major foundations to get together, take out some maps, and jointly create a time-and-space strategy to create a web of deeper learning exemplar schools in every part of the country within the next five years. I urge foundations to create a large nationwide fund to support schools in transition to assessment and reporting systems that measure a balance of academic and noncognitive student growth. Use the power of your purses and reputation to help break the dam of grades, test scores, and faulty college admissions practices that are hurting our kids and crippling innovation in our schools. Fund district- and site-level family education programs aimed at dispelling the myth of "elite colleges" and that help students and parents find and prepare for application to colleges that support "Turning the Tide" or similar public initiatives.

- *Connectivity* is the greatest nutrient of innovation, so I urge funders to put money where it will create greater connections among leading agents of change inside and outside of education. Set a goal that *all* of the 30 largest American cities will have city- or region-wide programs similar to Remake Learning in Pittsburgh. Fund leading educators, particularly those specializing in pedagogy, to work with companies developing VR for education. Imagine the impacts of free, relation-rich learning connections among diverse stakeholders around the world.

- Keep pushing to make learning *open and accessible* to teachers and their students. Prioritize bridge grants for materials and professional development to schools and districts that set rapid OER adoption goals. Join with the Hewlett Foundation and prioritize funding for the creation, sharing, and maintenance of fully accredited and free OER.

- Work with your college and university partners to rethink and build a fundamentally new relationship between postsecondary and K–12 education and the broader communities that they serve.

College and University Presidents, Admissions Officers, and Education and Business School Deans and Faculty Members

Colleges and universities intersect with K–12 education in two important ways, and they can become some of our most powerful positive agents of change. The first is in the college admissions process and how that steers student assessment and learning priorities. The second is as the teachers of our teachers. Colleges have a deservedly lofty place in the pantheon of global societies. They strongly influence what the rest of us consider "best practices." All colleges and universities, and particularly those that are household names in their region or nationally, can play a much larger and more important role in the critical evolution of K–12 education if they will get off the sidelines and place themselves squarely in the game.

We are starting to see some movement, but these institutions, filled as they are with talented, smart, dynamic people, have to get over their love of the status quo, their reverence for cloistered niches of research and publication, and take hold of the powerful role that they can play in shifting their own institutions and those of their K–12 family.

Among the major steps that colleges and universities can take in the next few years are the following:

- Sign on to the "Turning the Tide" consortium or adopt similar admissions policies and commit to those values, not just in theory but in actual practice. Publish your minimum entrance exam test scores and high school course requirements each year, and then guarantee that those metrics will not receive any additional weight in the admissions process. Publicly support development of new K–12 assessment and reporting strategies, such as the Mastery Transcript Consortium, and accept applicants from schools that use the new transcripts.

- Get out into the schools and communities near you. Find out what K–12 stakeholders need for effective student learning when we take away the singular goals of high test scores and test-based college admissions. Then, fundamentally rethink schools of education and business to meet those needs. Incentivize faculty members who model deeper learning practices in their own teaching. Support education school faculty members who require, or at least offer, on-site practicums or other hands-on experiences at deeper learning-type schools in your area. Rebuild your teacher accreditation systems on competency, not the number of units a candidate survives.

- Gather state and regional leadership groups together and *lead* expansive, forward-leaning, imagination and design sessions with diverse stakeholder groups of public and private school teachers, administrators, faculty, and students, business leaders, and accreditation organizations. Lead and anchor school-community partnerships that breach the boundary between K–12 schools and the rich learning resources in the communities around them. Create incentives for top faculty members in education and business to lead hands-on teacher training partnerships. Incentivize social science, education, and business faculty and graduate students to research the long-term success, obstacles, and impacts of school-community partnerships.

- Take the lead in building a system of education on the pillar of open access to knowledge. Leap on board the OER bandwagon; college textbooks are some of the most expensive compilations of the written word on the planet. Provide tangible incentives to faculty members who use or assist in the publication of OER at college and K–12 levels. If you have a school or department of education that trains teachers, insist that they offer instruction in how to use OER in K–12 learning.

The Fourth Estate

Finally, there is a significant role for the 21st century members of the "fourth estate": journalists, authors, and social media activists. We live in a world that increasingly relies on social, not commercial, connections. What we know and believe does not need to be restrained by mythologies of the past. But there are powerful interests that wish to preserve that past, who benefit from a lack of knowledge and transparency. It is painful that this should be the case in an institution—education—that should be wholly dedicated to the interests of our children, but that is the reality. In any modern revolution, the fourth estate has played an important part, sometimes ethically and sometimes decidedly not so. I urge these important actors to play a positive role by focusing attention on the successes around them and holding leaders accountable for progress toward their goals.

- Give in-depth coverage of schools and districts that are building nontraditional school-community partnerships. Record and share video interviews and short documentary evidence that show how these partnerships operate and offer an expanded student experience.
- Hold colleges and universities accountable for their public statements about the admissions process. Publish case studies and share research on how college admissions reflect (or not) their published policies.
- Research and publish stories on the use of open educational resources. Focus on cost savings and waste and the control currently exercised by the textbook publishing oligarchy.

CHAPTER TEN

Let's Roll

The education revolution will not *be authorized!*
              Kaleb Rashad, principal, High Tech High School

*So we can't go backward, we can only go where the evolutionary trajectory is
taking us and attune our ideas about ourselves and our existence to that course.*
                                    Thom Mayne, architect

*Malcolm Gladwell (2004) tells a wonderful story of how, in the 1980s, the Campbell's
company, maker of Prego spaghetti sauce, just could not figure out why they were getting completely thrashed by their rival Ragu. (Nod to my colleague Tim Fish, chief
innovation officer at the National Association of Independent Schools, for pointing me
to Gladwell's story.) They brought the problem to renowned consumer expert Harold
Moskowitz, who set out on a nationwide crusade to find the answer. He worked with
the Campbell's chefs to create 40 different kinds of spaghetti sauce with every variation
of spices and tomatoes and thickness and ingredients, and then he had thousands of
people taste samples and rate them. What he found, says Gladwell, was that Americans
basically fell into three groups in terms of the kinds of spaghetti sauce they like: regular,
spicy, and extra chunky. The problem was that there was no such thing as extra chunky
spaghetti sauce. So Prego created that line of products and in 10 years sold $600 mil-
lion of extra chunky sauce. It is not a coincidence that we now have market aisles lined*

with dozens of varieties of spaghetti and barbecue sauces that did not exist 20 years ago and that coffee shops dot every downtown selling a mind-numbing number of variations of a ground-up bean.

What Is Your Extra Chunky?

The point is that many of us don't know what we want until we see, feel, hear, or taste it, and that is absolutely the case in education. We were all brought up thinking that there was one kind of education sauce, or one kind of education coffee, to continue the analogies. We thought *that* product was the best because we were told it was the best, and we proved it to ourselves by seeing that our students got good grades and were accepted at good colleges . . . except for the large portions of the population who did not.

Now we are able to see, feel, and understand that what we want is something very different, a system of education that is engaging and relevant; tailored to students as individuals, not as artificial calculations of "average"; that prepares them to live, work, and be happy in a world that does not at all operate within the physical and conceptual confines of the cloistered walls and halls of the school we went to when we were kids. We want something extra chunky and we are going to get it, either at our neighborhood school or elsewhere. Not all but many stakeholders want schools to look more like the examples in this book, and they are willing to press on levers that might be bold and audacious because the intersection of need and opportunity is so profound. So pick a lever or all of them, and press hard. We *can* jump-start the new education operating system in just a few years. If we don't, it is our own damn fault, because there is nothing stopping us from building and pressing these levers.

Not all but many stakeholders want schools to look more like the examples in this book, and they are willing to press on levers that might be bold and audacious because the intersection of need and opportunity is so profound

Springtime in the Desert

When I launched the idea of my last book, *#EdJourney,* I had to get in my Prius and drive around the country for the entire fall 2012 to intersect with a trove of innovative schools. My home region, densely populated Southern California, was, with the exception of one or two notable oases, a desert of school innovation. I recognize that in this book I cited a number of examples from close to home, and that is neither a coincidence nor laziness on my part. In the past three years, a perfect storm of education innovation has begun to brew in San Diego County, the kind of storm that any city or region can replicate. The key lesson from what we are seeing in the county is this: Evolution and revolution need that critical density of forward-leaning school leaders and school examples, and then the oases begin to rapidly coalesce into wide, green fields.

In 2014, the only school in the San Diego region with any real "innovation gravity" was High Tech High. By 2016 all of that had changed. Design 39 Campus opened with a bang of public attention, and as of this writing is still overwhelmed with outside visitors taking two-hour student-led tours every week. The founding team of Vista Innovation Design Academy mashed up with the team from D39C, received deserved national attention, and now Vista Unified has won one of the 10 prestigious XQ America Challenge awards. Cajon Valley Union District, Del Lago Academy, E3 Civic High, Quantum Academy Val Verde District just to the north in Riverside County, Bayside STEAM Academy in Imperial Beach . . . the list of schools shifting to a truly deeper learning model is expanding more quickly than I can track.

What was the catalyst? What creates the conditions for a city or region to make that leap from fear to the rush of excitement and awareness that won't be squelched by the inevitable jitters of failure and criticism? It sure is not a top-down mandate from some all-knowing and all-powerful school innovation czar! And it is not something that happens only when the rain of more money falls on parched ground; California per-student expenditures in public schools are now among the lowest in the country. It comes down to an initial group of people who create the conditions that enable others to see, touch, and share what great learning can look like. In the case of San Diego County, that started with the courageous teacher leaders of Design 39 Campus and VIDA who visited High Tech High and Middle; collectively pulled in district and community support; cajoled friends; pinched pennies; and then offered an open-to-all one-day FutureNow Edu conference in 2015, for which more than 150 educators showed up. The next year they held two one-day conferences with different themes, and more than 400 educators attended, with teachers traveling from as far away as Canada and Colorado to participate. The Design Camp San Diego in 2017 "sold out" to more than 300 participants in less than a week, and the only advertising was via social media.

> *It comes down to an initial group of people who create the conditions that enable others to see, touch, and share what great learning can look like.*

The events are free or nearly so. There are no expensive keynoters (I know because I waive my fees when invited), lunch is either a bring-your-own brown bag or box lunch donated by a sponsor, and all of the breakout sessions are provided by peers for free. There is little lofty theory espoused at these events; they are focused on "what can I do in my classroom with my students tomorrow" to create a deeper learning experience. Those hundreds of teachers, supported by their principals and superintendents, go back to their schools, and within just a few years, the oases have turned into a growing number of green fields. All of this can be replicated, right now in your city, town, or region. Just reach out to the people I have introduced you to in this book, and they will be happy to share how you, too, can help the desert to bloom!

The Bad, Good, and Great News

In order to change a system, we need to be, well, systematic about it. As I quoted Larry Singer in Chapter Two, a lever without a place to slot into the system is just a club we are waving in the air. Shifting the metaphor from machinery to ecosystems, which is where I hope the direction education is moving, we can take a whole bucket of chemicals and biological bits and pieces and toss it into a warm pond, but we aren't suddenly going to get DNA, let alone pollywogs. Systems evolve through synergistic and sustained application of forces and resources. In other words, hoping is not going to get us there.

The only *really* bad news accrues to those who have the capacity to contribute, to find and press levers, and just don't because it is too uncomfortable or because those levers are going to interfere with self-interest. As I noted at the outset, some communities don't have current capacity to lean on these levers right now because of the crippling inequities of poverty and social structures. Some school communities that fall into those categories press the levers anyway, and when they move the system we all rejoice extra loudly. But for those who can choose to solve the problems and don't, I think the future is not rosy.

The great news that I hope readers take away from this book is that education does not need to remain stuck in the past. There are many, many examples of individuals, schools, and districts that have found ways to push past the crippling inertia that has imprisoned so many others in a system that no longer meets the needs of our children. The *really* great news is that none of us have to do it all on our own. Education holds *the* biggest lever of actual innovation, something that even Silicon Valley doesn't have. We are *the best* when it comes to sharing and stealing. We freely share and steal with and from each other all the time; we *want* to give away what works best! All we need is the effective density to do that, not impersonally by posting to some website, but personally, where we can ask questions and get answers from other real, practicing peers who are solving the same problems we face.

> *Education holds the biggest lever of actual innovation, something that even Silicon Valley doesn't have. We are the best when it comes to sharing and stealing.*

Finally, Trajectory

Think for a moment about how scientists at NASA compute the trajectory of a rocket that must intersect a planet or a moon or an asteroid 3, 5, or 10 years from now. They need to calculate an extraordinarily clear and precise understanding of where that rock is going to be in the vastness of

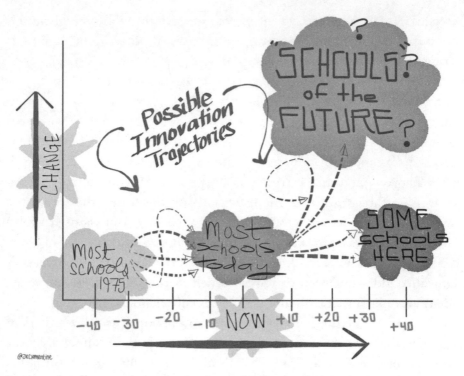

Is your school on a trajectory to intersect the future of education?
Art credit: Jolina Clement

space at some distant point in the future, and they need to have an equally clear understanding of how the rocket will launch and maintain a precise trajectory. They know they will not be perfect, that they might need fuel on board to make some mid-course corrections. And they know that changes in trajectory earlier in the mission are vastly less severe than changes they might have to make as the vessel approaches its target. If they wait too long, the changes needed to hit the target become more and more radical, and finally, at some point, impossible. They miss.

Some schools and communities are on a trajectory that will intersect the future needs of their students. Most schools and communities are not. Most are still on a trajectory that assumes that the future of education, in fact the future of our human society, 10 or 20 years from now looks pretty much like it does today. They are hoping or betting that the inevitable is actually improbable. Those are hollow hopes and very risky bets, and the stakes they are gambling with are our kids. The longer we wait to make the adjustments needed to intersect the future, the more likely we will miss that target, in which case our schools will cease to be the powerful, relevant force that they have been in the past.

The longer we wait to make the adjustments needed to intersect the future, the more likely we will miss that target, in which case our schools will cease to be the powerful, relevant force that they have been in the past.

What does success at scale look like in the great transformation ahead? How will school systems know that they have arrived at the future, that their trajectory has been true? How will we know that many or most of our schools have adopted a post–industrial age model of deeper learning? How will we know, as I outlined in Chapter One, if or when a new "operating system" has been adopted across big chunks of the K–12 education landscape?

We won't. The future does not come in a can or with an instruction manual. There will not be a single point in time when we can say, "switch over to the new operating system," as if we were rebooting our laptop. There will, however, be a tipping point, when a quantum number of educational innovators have shifted the learning practice at enough schools; when the demand of families for education relevant to this century and not the last have resulted in the closing of unresponsive traditional schools; when colleges and universities have adjusted their antiquated, test-based admissions policies; when many, if not all, students across the social and economic arc of the nation actually have equitable access to education; when communities, and in particular the business community that thrives only when there is a strong pipeline of students prepared to join them, are active participants in the world of K–12 education; when students don't think of school as someplace apart from the rest of their lives; when knowledge is not a purchased commodity; when the passion to learn and grow is not confined by walls or slave to daily schedules.

We won't know that time until it is on us. I believe we are much closer than most of us think.

VALUABLE AND CITED WEBSITES

Introduction

Deeper Learning Network
http://deeperlearning4all.org/deeper-learning-in-schools

Edutopia
https://www.edutopia.org/

Hewlett Foundation
http://www.hewlett.org/

EE Ford Foundation
https://www.eeford.org/

Institute for the Future of Learning
http://www.the-ifl.org/

Woodrow Wilson Foundation
http://woodrow.org/

Chapter 1

Transforming Teaching Project
http://www.totransformteaching.org/

EdLeader21
http://www.edleader21.com/

XQ America Challenge
https://xqsuperschool.org/

Convergence Center for Policy Resolution
http://www.convergencepolicy.org/

Transcend Education
http://www.transcendeducation.org/

High Tech High Schools
http://www.hightechhigh.org/

Big Picture Learning Network
http://www.bigpicture.org/

Chapter 2

Albermarle County School District
https://www2.k12albemarle.org/Pages/default.aspx

Cajon Valley Union School District
http://www.cajonvalley.net/

Vista Unified School District
http://www.vistausd.org/

Vista Innovation and Design Academy
http://vida.vistausd.org/

Elizabeth Forward School District
http://www.efsd.net/pages/Elizabeth_Forward

Riverpoint Academy
http://riverpoint.mead354.org/

Chapter 3

Design Lab Early College High School
http://www.clevelandmetroschools.org/designlab

Tools at Schools
http://www.tools-at-schools.com/

Thinkabit Lab
https://www.thinkabitlab.com/

Design Tech High School
http://www.designtechhighschool.org/

Remake Learning Network
http://remakelearning.org/

Holy Family Academy
https://www.hfa-pgh.org/?wssl=1

Center for Advanced Research and Technology (CART)
http://cart.org/

Lab Atlanta
http://www.labatlanta.org/

Progressive Education Network
https://progressiveeducationnetwork.org/

Cornerstone Academy for Social Action Middle School
http://schools.nyc.gov/SchoolPortals/11/X462/default.htm

Nanakuli School
http://nhis.nwcomplex.org/

Chapter 4

Wolfram Alpha
https://www.wolframalpha.com/

Eureka Math
https://greatminds.org/math

EngageNY
https://www.engageny.org/

K–12 OER Collaborative
http://openupresources.org/

UnboundED
https://www.unbounded.org/

Education First
http://education-first.com/

CK–12 Foundation
http://www.ck12.org/

Chapter 5

Mt. Vernon Institute for Innovation
http://www.mvifi.org/

Next Generation Learning Challenges
http://nextgenlearning.org/

Coalition for Access, Affordability, and Success
http://www.coalitionforcollegeaccess.org/members.html

California Multi-Trade Partnership
http://www.cde.ca.gov/nr/ne/yr16/yr16rel40.asp

Mastery Transcript Consortium
http://www.mastery.org/

Next Generation Learning Challenges
http://nextgenlearning.org/

Chapter 6

Woodrow Wilson Academy of Teaching and Learning
http://woodrowacademy.org/

High Tech High Graduate School of Education
http://gse.hightechhigh.org/

Deans for Impact
https://deansforimpact.org/

Sanford Inspire Program, Arizona State University
http://sanfordinspireprogram.org/

Bill and Melinda Gates Foundation
http://www.gatesfoundation.org/

Harvard Graduate School of Education
http://www.gse.harvard.edu/

Chapter 7

High Fidelity, Inc.
https://highfidelity.io/

Virbela
http://virbela.com/

Microsoft Hololens
https://www.microsoft.com/microsoft-hololens/en-us

Google Expeditions
https://www.google.com/edu/expeditions/

Bayside STEM Academy
http://bayside.smfcsd.net/

Education Reimagined
http://www.convergencepolicy.org/latest-projects/k-12-education-reform/

Chapter 8

Center for Transformational Leadership
https://www.smu.edu/Simmons/CommunityEnrichment/Leadership-Impact/Education

Science Leadership Academy
https://scienceleadership.org/

EduCon
http://2017.educon.org/

Deeper Learning Conference
http://www.deeper-learning.org/dl2017/index.php

University of Virginia's Darden School of Business and the Curry School of Education
http://www.darden.virginia.edu

University of Pennsylvania, the School Leadership Program
http://www2.gse.upenn.edu/slp

Next Gen Leadership Academy, University of Kentucky
http://sites.education.uky.edu/nxgla

Wisconsin CESA 1
http://www.cesa1.k12.wi.us/programs/

BIBLIOGRAPHY

Astin, A. *Are You Smart Enough? How Colleges' Obsession with Smartness Shortchanges Students* (Sterling, VA: Stylus Publishing, 2016).

Bliss, T., and S. Patrick. "OER State Policy in K–12 Education: Benefits, Strategies, and Recommendations for Open Access, Open Sharing." International Association for K–12 Online Learning. 2016. www.inacol.org/wp-content/uploads/2015/02/oer-state-policy.pdf.

Boston Consulting Group. "Teachers Know Best: Teachers' Views on Professional Development." 2014. https://s3.amazonaws.com/edtech-production/reports/Gates-PDMarketResearch-Dec5.pdf.

Catmul, E. *Creativity, Inc.* (New York: Random House Center for Public Education, 2014). www.nsba.org/tags/center-public-education.

Chomsky, N. "Interview with *The Progressive*," YouTube. 2015. www.youtube.com/watch?v=9JVVRWBekYo.

Cogshall, J. "Title II, Part A: Don't Scrap It, Don't Dilute It, FIX IT." American Policy Center of the American Institutes of Research. March 2015. http://educationpolicy.air.org/sites/default/files/FixItBrief.pdf.

Council of Chief State School Officers. "State of the States: Open Educational Resources in K–12 Education." November 2014. www.ccsso.org/Documents/2014/Open%20Educational%20Resources%20in%20K–12%20Education-ver1.1.pdf.

Csikszentmihalyi, M. *Flow: The Psychology of Optimal Experience* (New York: Harper Collins, 1990).

Darling Hammond, L., R. Wei, A. Andree, N. Richardson, and S. Orphanos. "Professional Learning in the Learning Profession: A Status Report on Teacher Development in the United States and Abroad" (Stamford, CT.: National Staff Development Council, February 2009).

Derisiewicz, W. *Excellent Sheep: The Miseducation of the American Elite and the Way to a Meaningful Life* (New York: Free Press, 2014).

Dintersmith, T., and T. Wagner. *Most Likely to Succeed* [film]. n.d. www.mltsfilm.org/.

Friedman, T. *Thank You for Being Late: An Optimist's Guide to Thriving in the Age of Accelerations* (New York: Farrar, Straus, and Giroux, 2016).

Frieze, D. "How I Became a Localist." TEDx Talk. 2015. http://tedxtalks.ted.com/video/ How-I-Became-a-Localist-Deborah.

Giancoloa, J., and R. Kahlenberg. "True Merit." Jack Kent Cooke Foundation. January 2016. www.jkcf.org/assets/1/7/JKCF_True_Merit_Report.pdf.

Gladwell, M. "Choice, Happiness, and Spaghetti Sauce." TED Talk. 2004. www.ted.com/ talks/malcolm_gladwell_on_spaghetti_sauce?language=en.

Govindarajan, V., and C. Trimble. *How Stella Saved the Farm* (New York: St. Martin's Press, 2013).

Hagel III, J., J. Seely Brown, and L. Davison. "Abandon Stocks; Embrace Flows." *Harvard Business Review.* January 27, 2009. https://hbr.org/2009/01/abandon-stocks-embrace-flows.html.

Isaccson, W. *The Innovators: How a Group of Hackers, Geniuses, and Geeks Created the Digital Revolution* (New York: Simon and Schuster, 2014).

Kamanetz, A. *The Test: Why Our Schools Are Obsessed with Standardized Testing—But You Don't Have to Be* (New York: Public Affairs/Perseus Books Group, 2015).

Lehmann, C., and Z. Chase. *Building School 2.0: How to Create the Schools We Need* (San Francisco: Jossey-Bass, 2015).

Lichtman, G. *#EdJourney: A Roadmap to the Future of Education* (San Francisco: Josey-Bass, 2014).

Lichtman, G. "Design of Schools and The Nature of Design, via Dr. Adrian Bejan: A Fascinating Read. January 2013a. www.grantlichtman.com/design-of-schools-and-the-nature-of-design-via-dr-adrian-bejan-a-fascinating-read/.

Lichtman, G. "Response from Dr. Adrian Bejan on Design of Nature." January 2013b. www.grantlichtman.com/response-from-dr-adrian-bejan-on-design-of-nature/.

Lichtman, G. "Rebuilding the K-12 Operating System." 2015. www.totransformteaching. org/rebuilding-the-k12-operating-system/.

Luthar, S., S. Barkin, and E. Crossman. "'I Can, Therefore I Must': Fragility in the Upper-Middle Classes." *Development and Psychopathology* 25 (2013): 1529–49.

Marcinek, A. "Transitioning to Open Educational Resources." *Edutopia.* March 8, 2013. www .edutopia.org/blog/transitioning-to-open-educational-resources-andrew-marcinek.

National Center on Addiction and Substance Abuse at Columbia University (CASAColumbia). "National Survey of American Attitudes on Substance Abuse XVII: Teens." 2012. www.casacolumbia.org/templates/publications_reports.aspx?keywords=2012+teens.

National School Boards Association. "Center for Public Education Study Finds the Path to Career Readiness." 2016. www.nsba.org/newsroom/press-releases/ center-public-education-study-finds-path-career-readiness.

Opfer, V., J. Kaufman, and L. Thompson. *Implementation of K–12 State Standards for Mathematics and English Language Arts and Literacy* (Santa Monica, CA: Rand Corporation, 2016).

Pentland, A. *Social Physics: How Social Networks Can Make Us Smarter* (New York: Penguin Press, 2014).

Porter, M. "Clusters and the New Economics of Competition." *Harvard Business Review*. November–December 1998.

Putnam, R. *Our Kids: The American Dream in Crisis* (New York: Simon and Schuster, 2015).

"Remake Learning Playbook." Remake Learning Network. http://remakelearning.org/ playbook/.

Ritchhart, R. *Creating Cultures of Thinking* (San Francisco: Josey-Bass, 2015).

Rivkin, J., and others. "Partial Credit: How America's Superintendents See Business as a Partner." Harvard Business School. 2013. www.hbs.edu/competitiveness/ Documents/partial-credit.pdf.

Rose, T. *The End of Average: How We Succeed in a World That Values Sameness* (New York: Harper One, 2015).

Rosin, H. "The Silicon Valley Suicides." *Atlantic Monthly*. December 2015.

"State of America's Schools: The Path to Winning Again in Education." Gallup Education. 2014. www.gallup.com/services/178769/state-america-schools-report.aspx.

Thinnes, C. "Public Schools at the Crossroads of Deeper Learning and Social Justice." *Special Needs Digest*. March 12, 2016. www.specialneedsdigest.com/2016/03/ learning-happens-everywhere-public.html.

Thompson, D. "The Thing Employers Look for When Hiring Recent Graduates." *Atlantic Monthly*. August 2014.

Tough, P. *Helping Children Succeed: What Works and Why* (Boston: Houghton Mifflin Harcourt, 2016).

Wiley, D., J. Hilton, S. Ellington, and T. Hall. "A Preliminary Examination of the Cost Savings and Learning Impacts of Using Open Textbooks in Middle and High School Science Classes." *The International Review of Research in Open and Distance Learning*, 2012. http://files.eric.ed.gov/fulltext/EJ1001022.pdf.

William and Flora Hewlett Foundation. "Deeper Learning Defined." April 2013. www. hewlett.org/library/deeper-learning-defined/.

Weissbourd, R., et al. "Turning the Tide." Harvard Graduate School of Education. 2016. http://mcc.gse.harvard.edu/files/gse-mcc/files/20160120_mcc_ttt_execsummary_ interactive.pdf.

INDEX